Genealogy Chart

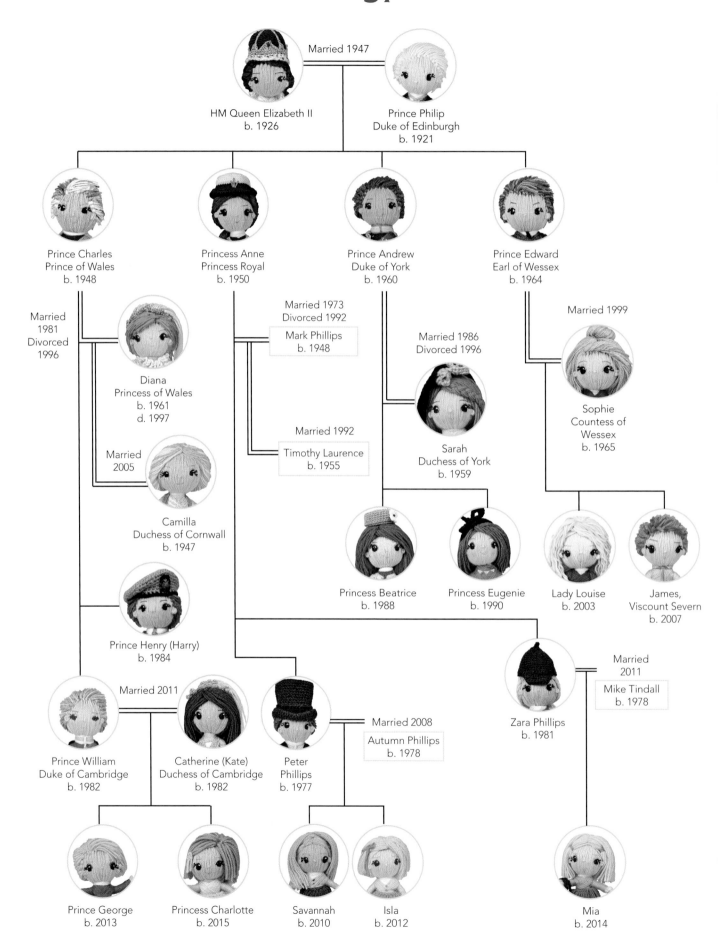

Married 1947

HM Queen Elizabeth II
b. 1926

Prince Philip
Duke of Edinburgh
b. 1921

Prince Charles
Prince of Wales
b. 1948

Princess Anne
Princess Royal
b. 1950

Prince Andrew
Duke of York
b. 1960

Prince Edward
Earl of Wessex
b. 1964

Married 1973
Divorced 1992

Mark Phillips
b. 1948

Married 1986
Divorced 1996

Married 1999

Married
1981
Divorced
1996

Diana
Princess of Wales
b. 1961
d. 1997

Married 1992

Timothy Laurence
b. 1955

Sarah
Duchess of York
b. 1959

Sophie
Countess of
Wessex
b. 1965

Married
2005

Camilla
Duchess of Cornwall
b. 1947

Princess Beatrice
b. 1988

Princess Eugenie
b. 1990

Lady Louise
b. 2003

James,
Viscount Severn
b. 2007

Prince Henry (Harry)
b. 1984

Married
2011

Mike Tindall
b. 1978

Married 2011

Zara Phillips
b. 1981

Married 2008

Autumn Phillips
b. 1978

Prince William
Duke of Cambridge
b. 1982

Catherine (Kate)
Duchess of Cambridge
b. 1982

Peter
Phillips
b. 1977

Prince George
b. 2013

Princess Charlotte
b. 2015

Savannah
b. 2010

Isla
b. 2012

Mia
b. 2014

YARN WHIRLED

The Royal Family

EASY-TO-CRAFT YARN CHARACTERS

PAT OLSKI

DOVER PUBLICATIONS, INC.
MINEOLA, NEW YORK

Dedication

This book is dedicated, with so much love and admiration, to my mother, Joan, and my grandmother, Sylvia, who were two of the most dignified, creative, and accomplished career women that I have ever known. Their dauntless enthusiasm and expert mastery of so many skills, ranging from needlecraft to differential equations, continues to inspire me every day.

Acknowledgment

I would like to acknowledge the extraordinary contribution of time, effort, and talent by (in alphabetical order) Terri Geus, Vanessa Putt, and Marie Zaczkiewicz, and the dynamic team at Dover Publications. Without their labor and insight there would be no royal "Whirled." I would also like to acknowledge Brian Kraus for his willingness to pose yarn figures as if they were royalty, and his ability to photograph them as if they were human. And thank you to Charlie Young for a wonderful web cover shot.

Photography by Brian Kraus
Step-by-step photos by Cynthia Castellari

Copyright

Copyright © 2017 by Pat Olski
All rights reserved.

Bibliographical Note

Yarn Whirled™: The Royal Family is a new work,
first published by Dover Publications, Inc., in 2017.

Library of Congress Cataloging-in-Publication Data

Names: Olski, Pat, author.
Title: Yarn whirled. The royal family : easy-to-craft yarn characters/
Pat Olski ; photography by Brian Kraus
Description: Mineola, New York : Dover Publications, Inc., 2017.
Identifiers: LCCN 2017000202 | ISBN 9780486812007 (paperback) | ISBN
  0486812006 (paperback)
Subjects: LCSH: Soft toy making—Patterns. | Yarn. | Royal houses—Great
  Britain. | BISAC: CRAFTS & HOBBIES / Toymaking. | CRAFTS & HOBBIES /
  Stuffed Animals.
Classification: LCC TT174.3 .O474 2017 | DDC 745.592—dc23
LC record available at https://lccn.loc.gov/2017000202

Manufactured in the United States by LSC Communications
81200601   2017
www.doverpublications.com

Contents

The Patterns

PRINCE WILLIAM
and his brother, PRINCE HARRY

Introduction

As a lifetime stitcher, I think that being a "yarnophile" and being an Anglophile are inextricably intertwined. An incredible wealth of the most exquisite and original techniques in needlework history emanated from the small group of islands now known as the United Kingdom and the Republic of Ireland.

The United Kingdom is an incomparable resource for needle arts, from rugged cabled fisherman sweaters, magical Fair Isle color work, and gorgeous woven tartans, to the most ethereal Shetland lace and delicate Ayrshire white work embroidery. Yarn and threadwork have long enriched the society and economy of these islands, as evidenced by the medieval Bayeaux tapestry and, later, by the rich, scrolling Jacobean crewelwork.

The one element common to a majority of these fiber traditions is that the United Kingdom, historically, has had a singular climate and landscape that has made it a very hospitable place in which to raise sheep. Centuries of honed expertise and selective breeding have produced wool with some of the finest characteristics in the world.

When it was suggested that a theme for my next *Yarn Whirled* book could be the Royal Family, I jumped at the chance. The British Royal Family is part of a monarchy that has lasted for centuries. It represents a dignified and stately tradition in a mercurial world. Yarn and needlecraft represent equally venerable traditions that give us peace and joy, as well as an anchor in technology-driven times.

from Yarn to "Yarn Whirled"

Yarn is irresistible. It has it <u>all</u>—exquisite color, appealing texture, and most importantly, unlimited potential. It represents calm and creativity, productivity and relaxation. It is so enticing. Few people can walk by a skein of yarn on a table without wanting to touch it.

Inextricably tangled in its lure, I have used yarn to knit, crochet, embroider, needlepoint, knot rugs, felt, tat, macramé, weave, make pompoms and tassels, braids and temari balls, fringe, and cording. I experimented with some techniques, became expert at others. I was pretty confident that I had exhausted all of the possibilities in this medium. I have been very fortunate to have been able to have a career in the yarn industry, teaching and designing.

I thought I had sampled all of the applications, and that all that was left was for me to deepen my skill level, until . . .

As random as novel ideas often are, I was struck with the idea of making a yarn doll for a class that I was teaching to young elementary-school students. An exhaustive internet search did not unearth anything similar to what I had in mind. I decided to design my own doll.

In retrospect, this idea was actually a confluence of past memories, projects, and techniques. I have a fond recollection of a hand-crocheted hat made by my mother for me when I was six, which I only wanted to wear because it had simple tassels that were knotted to look like dolls at the end of the ties. As a child, I made dolls out of yarn, felt, clay, fabric, and beads. I had a decided mental image of what I wanted those dolls to look like, and rarely was I satisfied. When my friends started to have babies, I made a number of cloth dolls to give away. Later, as the mother of two boys, my doll-making career came to an abrupt end! As a designer, I have been asked to knit and crochet yarn toys for publication, and I have thoroughly enjoyed the experience—but until now, none of them were dolls.

When I first experimented with the yarn doll, my intent was to make nothing fancier than a glorified tassel with braided limbs—an idea that goes back to the pioneer corn-husk and straw dolls. But, as I worked on my first doll, I was amazed at how firm the yarn was when wrapped together, and I was surprised with the results. Different iterations yielded better and better outcomes. I couldn't believe how seamlessly the whole idea came together. When I disliked the original idea I had for a shoe, a quick trial with wrapping each side of the foot separately yielded a flexible, perfectly proportionate, foot, in a manner I couldn't have planned for if I had tried. The original dolls I created had a simple tie at each end of a bundle to create a hand. When I saw the strands of yarn lying smoothly on the board, the idea popped into my mind to try making a thumb. I thought the yarn would be too bulky and the thumb too fiddly, but yet again, I was pleasantly surprised.

The dolls in this book represent the forward progression of my techniques. I can only say that despite all of my planning and experience, it was the properties of the yarn itself that ultimately dictated the proportions and designs of these adorable characters, and that is really how "Yarn Whirled" was created.

QUEEN ELIZABETH II's CORONATION—JUNE 2, 1953

HM QUEEN ELIZABETH II and PRINCE PHILIP, Duke of Edinburgh

PRINCE CHARLES, Prince of Wales; QUEEN ELIZABETH II;
PRINCE GEORGE; PRINCE WILLIAM, Duke of Cambridge

Top row, left to right: PRINCE ANDREW, Duke of York;
PRINCESS ANNE, Princess Royal; PRINCE EDWARD, Earl of Wessex
Bottom row, left to right: PRINCE PHILIP, Duke of Edinburgh;
QUEEN ELIZABETH II; PRINCE CHARLES, Prince of Wales

DIANA
Princess of Wales
(1961–1997)

SARAH FERGUSON
Duchess of York

PRINCE EDWARD, Earl of Wessex, and
SOPHIE, Countess of Wessex

PRINCE CHARLES and
CAMILLA,
Duchess of Cornwall

QUEEN ELIZABETH and PRINCE PHILIP with Their Eight Grandchildren

Front row, left to right: LADY LOUISE WINDSOR; JAMES, VISCOUNT SEVERN

Back row, left to right: PRINCE WILLIAM, PETER PHILLIPS, PRINCESS BEATRICE, ZARA PHILLIPS TINDALL, PRINCESS EUGENIE, PRINCE HARRY

CATHERINE,
Duchess of Cambridge, and

PRINCE WILLIAM,
Duke of Cambridge

QUEEN ELIZABETH with her Five Great-Grandchildren and
Two Youngest Grandchildren

Front row, left to right: JAMES, VISCOUNT SEVERN; MIA TINDALL;
PRINCESS CHARLOTTE; PRINCE GEORGE; ISLA PHILLIPS
Back row, left to right: LADY LOUISE, SAVANNAH PHILLIPS

PRINCESS BEATRICE
and her sister,
PRINCESS EUGENIE

LADY LOUISE WINDSOR
and her brother,
JAMES, VISCOUNT SEVERN

ZARA PHILLIPS TINDALL
and her brother, PETER PHILLIPS

Materials and Tips

Scissors

Sturdy, sharp scissors are a must to cut through the layers of yarn. Dull scissors will fray the edges of the yarn.

Needles

A blunt, smooth tapestry needle with an eye large enough for your yarn is a necessity. I keep an assortment of needles from size 13–16 on a magnet at my work space, so I have a place to park my needles while I work. I prefer metal needles.

But, why do I need a needle if I don't need to know how to sew to make these characters? Great question. The needle is used to bury the ends of yarn into the doll and to affix the hair to the head. You can knot the hairpiece to the head and use a crochet hook to pull the yarn ends into an inconspicuous place. However, a needle can do those things and more, and you will find it easier to use than the methods that I have just mentioned.

If you wish to stitch on the features, a needle is necessary. Nevertheless, there are many non-stitching facial-feature options for the truly needle-averse. You may paint, glue, or snap on the eyes, nose, and mouth. Craft stores are full of no-sew options for doll makers.

Rulers and tape measures

A good straight edge ruler is needed to measure and mark the center points on your board. A tape measure is necessary to measure the circumference of an object, such as the ball of yarn used to fill the head.

Powder blush

I use my fingertip to smooth on powder blush in a circle on the cheeks. It is remarkably long-lasting, and the powder covers the unevenness of the yarn.

Choosing a board

You will need a board made of cardboard, wood, or plastic to wrap the yarn around. Pieces of mat board or corrugated cardboard glued together work well. The dimensions are stated with each pattern. Just be certain that the board has smooth edges so that the yarn will not snag and that the board is sturdy enough so it does not bend, buckle, or snap from the pressure of the wrapped yarn. Use a permanent marker to mark the center point of each edge.

Yarn

To my surprise and delight, I have had success with all types of yarn, from synthetics to natural fiber. When you select yarn for the body of the doll, choose a yarn that is strong enough to be wrapped with a certain degree of tension. I believe that the firmness and evenness of the resulting wraps is more important than the composition of the fiber. When using wool, my preference is to use superwash treated wool for the body, because it has a slightly smoother appearance than untreated wool. Test the yarn for strength and appearance by wrapping it around your fingers. Some yarns form lovely smooth wraps, and some look rather rope-y. Depending upon your yarn choices and your own yarn wrap tension, you may need to make fewer or additional wraps to have complete coverage. As a rule of thumb, each large doll that is wrapped completely in the body color takes about 180–200yds/165m–183m of a DK–worsted weight yarn in the body/head color to complete.

This is the perfect craft to make use of novelty yarns with unusual texture and fiber. Every fiber from silk to raffia has a unique appearance and can only enhance your finished character. Trendy ruffle, net, and fabric yarns are perfect for quick coverage and unusual effects. The only caveat would be to save the more fragile yarns for the clothing and embellishments.

Key Points for Success

* Do not wrap your yarn too tightly. You do not want the board to buckle, bend, or break. With practice you should be able to make smooth, even wraps.

* Remember, as crazy as this seems, you may be building muscles in your hands you are not used to using. With time, the wrapping and twisting will not be tiring.

* The "order of operations" that I have detailed in the basic directions is the one that worked best for me. It is easiest to wrap the shoes and legs before making the head.

* You will be surprised at how little the yarn "unwinds" while you are working with it. However, if you are concerned, you may always tape down loose ends while you have pieces set aside—for instance, the thumbs—until you pick them up to work on them again.

* Save your yarn scraps. They are perfect to use to fill the center of the yarn ball that is used to stuff the head. Be sure to wrap this yarn ball very firmly.

* Threading a thick yarn into a tapestry needle can be a feat. So, I suggest wrapping the yarn around the eye of the needle, pinching the bend firmly, and then trying to thread the bend through the eye. It takes some practice, but it really works. If you are working with a novelty yarn, you may wish to fold a tiny piece of paper over the end of the yarn and then insert the paper-covered yarn end into the needle.

* After I have embroidered the eyes, I wet the eyelash floss and use the tip of my tapestry needle to fan out the eyelashes. Once they are dry, I trim them.

* Once the doll is finished, I give it a haircut. Because the hair consists of layers of yarn, you may need to move the hair gently and trim the ends a few times until you are satisfied.

QUEEN ELIZABETH
and PRINCE PHILIP

Getting Started with Step-by-Step Techniques

Wind yarn around board for desired number of wraps to make a bundle.

Constrictor Knot

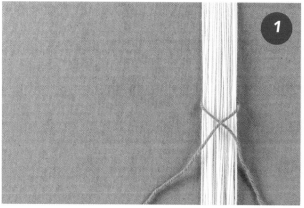

1. Fold yarn piece in half. Place yarn under bundle, with halfway point centered. Bring right and left tails to front. Cross the tails over the front of the bundle, right over left (facing you).

2. Wrap the right tail around the back of the work, under the bundled yarn.

3. Bring to front under the left tail.

4. Bring yarn over the left tail and slide it under the previously made cross.

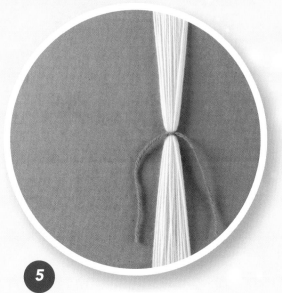

Finished bundle tied on one side with a constrictor knot.

Lark's Head Knot

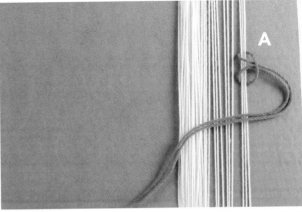

Fold knot yarn(s) in half. Slide loop (A) under the foundation (wrapped) yarn.

Take 2 cut ends of knot yarn, fold them over foundation (wrapped) yarn, and then insert them into loop (A) created at top of bend. Pull gently.

1

Use a series of Lark's Head Knots to secure a wrapped fringe, as for a wig.

2

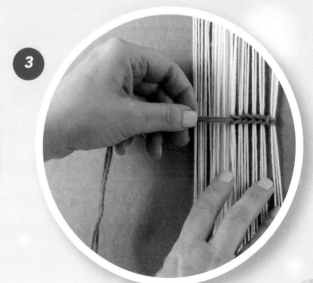

3

Arm Bundle

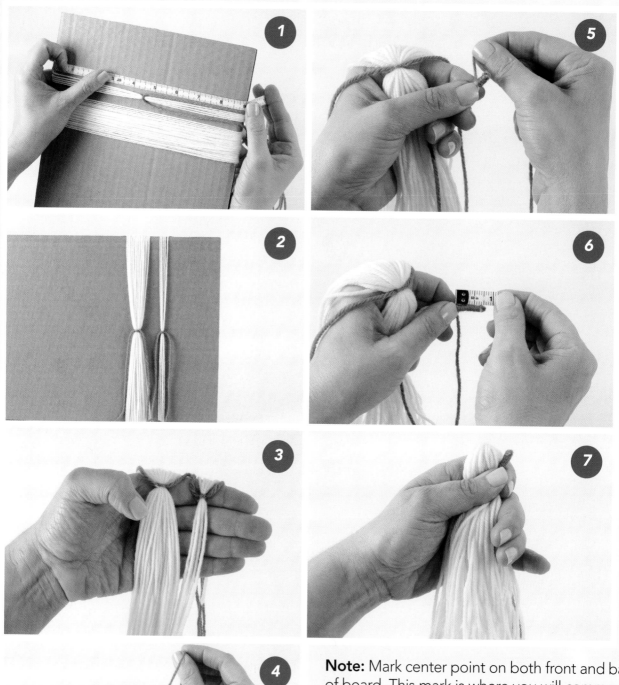

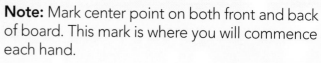

Note: Mark center point on both front and back of board. This mark is where you will commence each hand.

1. Knot at top of doll's thumb.

2. Knot at top of doll's hand.

3. Remove from board.

4–5. Pinch and wrap thumb.

6. Completed thumb.

7. Pinch thumb and hand at wrist.

Arm Bundle

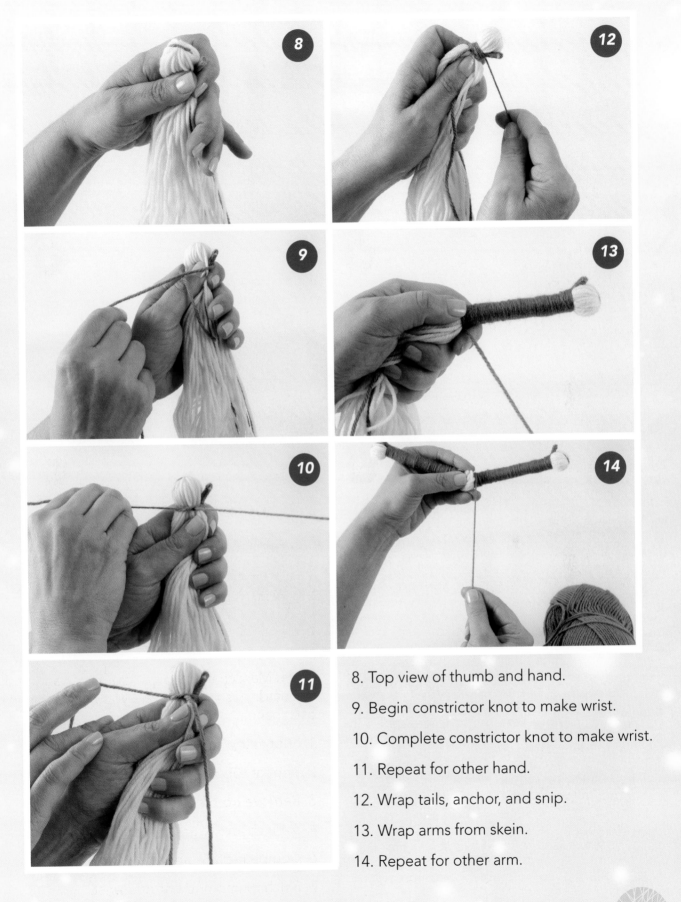

8. Top view of thumb and hand.

9. Begin constrictor knot to make wrist.

10. Complete constrictor knot to make wrist.

11. Repeat for other hand.

12. Wrap tails, anchor, and snip.

13. Wrap arms from skein.

14. Repeat for other arm.

Head * Body * Leg Bundle (Make 2)

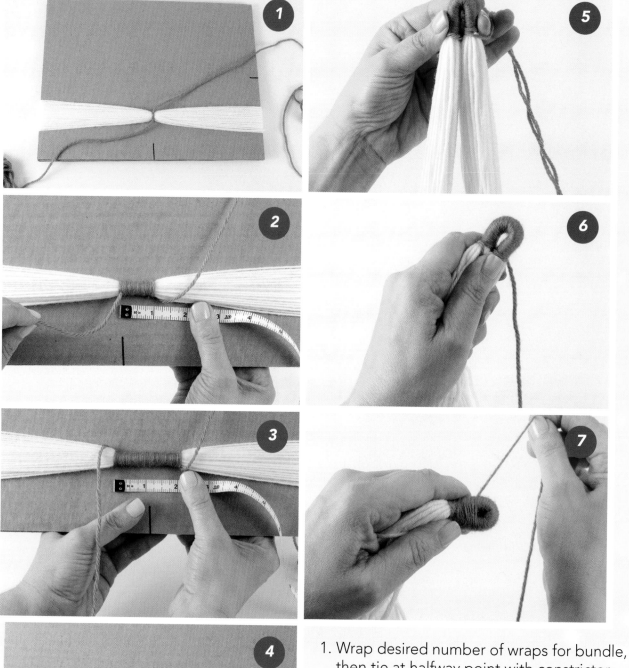

1. Wrap desired number of wraps for bundle, then tie at halfway point with constrictor knot to form center of shoe.

2. Wrap shoe yarn for one inch to right of knot.

3. Wrap shoe yarn for one inch to left of knot.

4. Flip board over. Make a temporary knot for top of head.

5. Remove bundle from board.

6. Bend shoe at center knot.

7. Wrap at bend to secure.

Head * Body * Leg Bundle

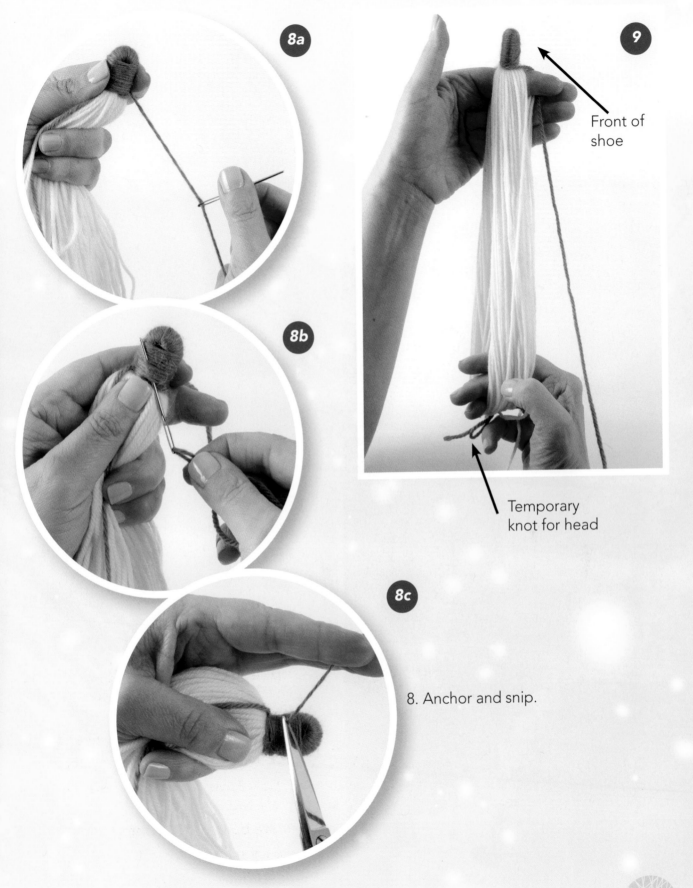

8a

9

Front of shoe

8b

Temporary knot for head

8c

8. Anchor and snip.

Head * Body * Leg Bundle

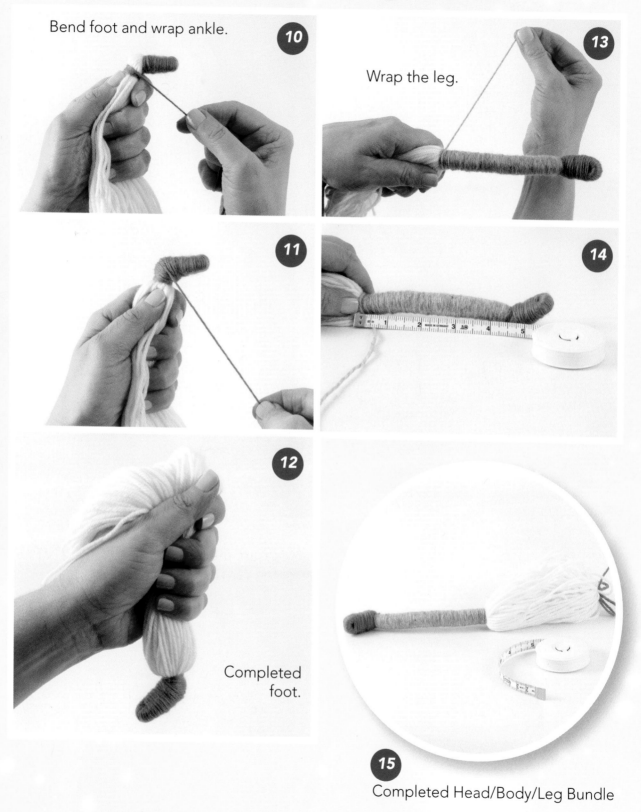

Bend foot and wrap ankle.

10

11

12

Completed foot.

Wrap the leg.

13

14

15

Completed Head/Body/Leg Bundle

Winding Yarn into a Ball

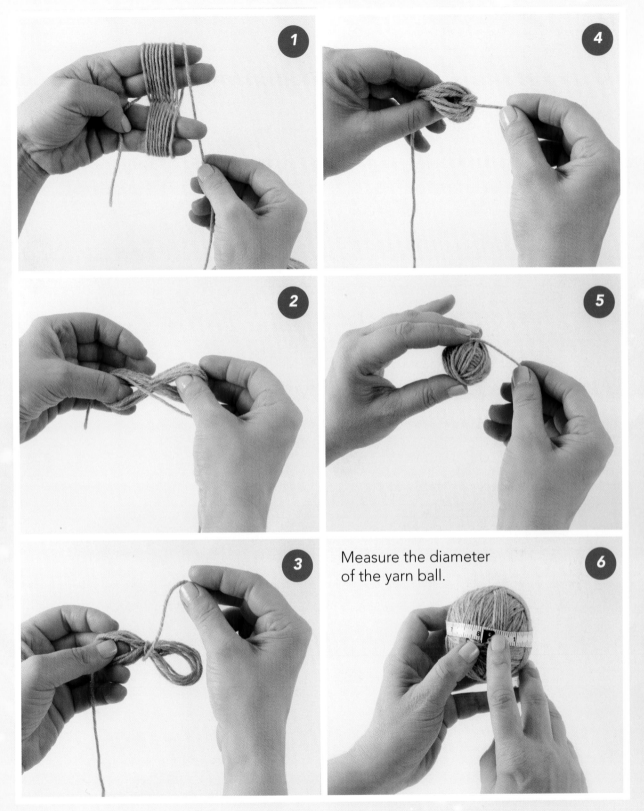

Measure the diameter
of the yarn ball.

Head * Body * Leg Bundle

1. Connect 2 Head/Body/Leg Bundles at top of head with knot.
2. Place ball of yarn inside head.
3. Place paper in between front and back to keep separate.
4. Insert arm bundle into body.
5. Tie a piece of yarn with constrictor knot at neck, and knot a piece of yarn under the arms for waist.
6. Attach and wrap shirt yarn from crotch over shoulders.

Head * Body * Leg Bundle

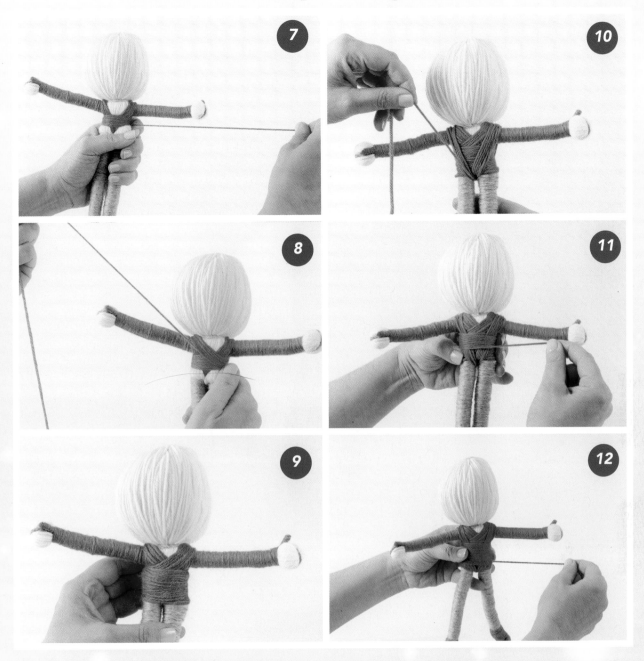

7. Wrap yarn around waist.

8. Wrap yarn from waist over shoulders.

9. Wrap yarn around waist and hips.

10–12. Repeat sequence until body is fully covered.

Hair Fringe

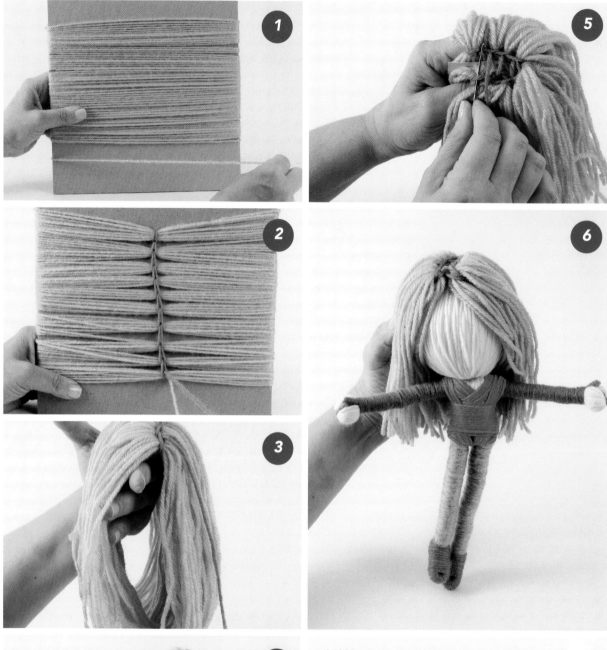

1. Wrap yarn.
2. Secure with Lark's Head Knots.
3. Remove from board, and cut at bottom.
4. Fold fringe in half, using a piece of paper to separate the sides.
5. Sew together at knots, creating a center part.
6. Doll with hair sewn onto head.

Hair Using Lark's Head Knot Method

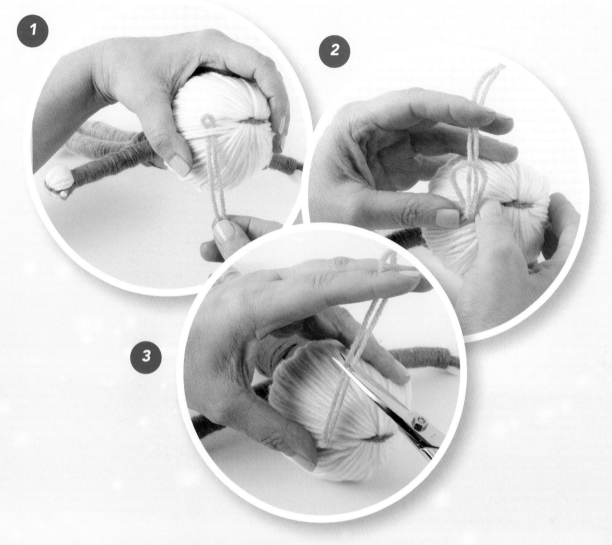

Cutting Off Loose Yarn Ends

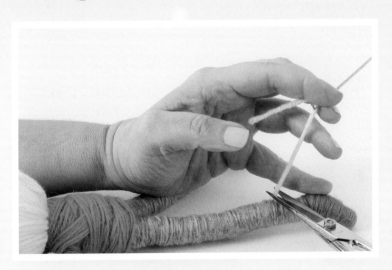

Basic Directions for the Large Doll

FINISHED HEIGHT Approximately 11in/28cm

MATERIALS

All figures require sharp scissors, a ruler, stiff cardboard, and a large, blunt-tipped tapestry needle. A stiff piece of paper is helpful to keep the strands of hair separate. A crochet hook will make it easier to form the knots on dolls with knotted-on hair.

Each pattern will specify the yarn that was used for the dolls in this book, but, of course, you can substitute yarn in a similar weight.

TECHNIQUE GLOSSARY

Anchor and Snip

Anchor all loose yarn ends by threading each end through the tapestry needle and burying it in the center of the bundle. Snip the excess.

Yarn Tail

Pieces of yarn on either side of a knot, or piece of yarn left at the end of a wrap.

Constrictor Knot

Fold the yarn in half. Place a piece of yarn under the bundle, with the halfway point centered. Bring the right and left tails to the front. Cross the tails over the front of the bundle, right over left. Wrap the right tail around the back of the work, then bring it to the front under the left tail, and then over the left tail and under the cross previously made. Pull both tails slowly until the knot is tight enough.

Lark's Head Knot

Fold the yarn piece(s) in half, creating a loop. Slide the loop under the foundation yarn. Take the cut ends of the yarn, fold them over the foundation yarn, and insert them into the loop created at the top of the bend. Pull gently. To make a fringe, cut the foundation yarn the length specified. Fold it in half and anchor it to a board. Tie the lark's head knots onto the yarn as specified in the individual directions.

DOLL

NOTE: Wrap the yarn evenly and smoothly, but not too tightly, around the board. You do not want the board to buckle, and you want to be able to remove the yarn bundle easily.

HEAD/BODY/LEG BUNDLE (Make 2)

Wrap the body-color yarn 65 times around a 12in/30.5cm board. Mark a line showing the center of the board. Cut the yarn from the skein.

MAKE THE SHOE

- Fold a 120in/305cm piece of shoe-color yarn in half, and mark the center. Slide the yarn under the wrapped yarn, lining up the center mark with the middle of the wrapped yarn. Tie a constrictor knot around the yarn at the center line of the board. There should be two tails each about 59in/150cm long. Wrap one tail around the bundle firmly and evenly for 1in/2.5cm, then wrap from the center line out in the other direction with the second yarn tail for 1in/2.5cm. Carefully remove the bundle from the board. Fold the bundle in half at the constrictor knot tie line, and wrap one yarn tail firmly around the shoe a number of times to secure; anchor the yarn end, and snip. Fold the foot at the ankle; wrap the remaining yarn tail around the ankle, then around the heel until all of the body yarn is covered. Anchor and snip.

- Use a 12in/30.5cm piece of yarn to loosely tie the other end of the bundle at the exact opposite end from the shoe, which will be for the head. This tie is temporary.

LEGS

- Wrap the legs with yarn directly from the skein†. Be sure to wrap the legs very firmly to give structure to the figure. Anchor the end and make a few very tight wraps at the ankle and then wrap up the leg for 4½in/11.5cm from the ankle and 5in/12.5cm from the bottom of the heel. Anchor and snip. Wrap the other leg to match, <u>making sure that the feet are both facing in the same direction.</u>

†The yarn color will be specified in the pattern. If no specific color is given, use MC. If done in a color other than the body color, this will create leggings or pants.

HEAD

- Take the two body bundles and thread a 12in/30.5cm piece of body yarn through both head pieces. Tie together firmly, using a constrictor knot. Make sure the knot is directly opposite the shoes. Remove the temporary ties.

- Wind a firm ball of body-color yarn that measures 2½in/6cm in diameter and 8in/20cm in circumference. You can economize by using scrap yarn inside the ball of yarn for the head, making sure to wrap a few layers of body-color yarn firmly over the scrap yarn.

- Place the ball inside the head bundle, smoothing the yarn and centering the ball carefully. Push the ball as high into the head as possible.

- Using a 12in/30.5cm piece of body yarn, firmly tie a constrictor knot for the neck, approximately 2¾in/7cm from the top of the head. Wrap the yarn tails smoothly around the neck. Smooth the head, making sure that the ball is centered and that the neck yarn is positioned firmly against the bottom of the yarn ball.

- Place a ruler or folded paper between the bundles to keep the front and back body yarn separate until the arm piece is completed.

ARM BUNDLE

- Wrap body-color yarn 45 times around a 9in/23cm board for the arms. Mark a line showing the center of the board. *At the center (4½in/11.5cm) mark, using a 12in/30.5cm piece of body yarn, make a constrictor knot to tie the five outer strands together for the thumb. Then, with a 12in/30.5cm piece of body-color yarn, firmly tie the remaining 40 strands together at the same point. Flip the board over and repeat from *. Be careful to center each knot so that the arms are the same length. Carefully remove from the board.

- To create the thumb, wrap one yarn tail from the thumb knot tightly around the five strands for about ¾in/2cm. Pinch the base of the thumb and hand together at the wrist and wrap the other yarn tail firmly and evenly around the thumb joint, and then tightly around the wrist.

- Working from the skein†, wrap the yarn firmly and evenly around the arm bundle until you have reached the center of the bundle. Repeat for the other side, making sure that the thumbs are both on the same side of the hand. Anchor, hide and snip all threads.

   †The yarn color will be specified in the pattern. If no specific color is given, use MC. If done in a color other than the body color, this will create sleeves.

BODY

- Insert the arm piece into the body bundles in the space under the head, being careful to keep the front and back strands separate. Cut an 18in/46cm piece of body yarn, and tie a constrictor knot firmly under the arm bundle, creating a waist. Make sure the arm bundle is centered and pressed firmly under the neck wrap.

- Using the yarn from the skein†, wrap the yarn evenly and smoothly eight times from the crotch (between the legs under the waist) to the right shoulder, and then eight times from the crotch to the left shoulder. Wrap the yarn 12 times from the waist down to define the hips, covering the previous work evenly. Wrap the yarn eight times from the left waist over the right shoulder, and then from the right waist over the left shoulder. Wrap the yarn 20 times around the body from the underarm to the hip, covering the previous work evenly. Wrap the yarn evenly and smoothly eight times from the crotch to the right shoulder, then eight times from the crotch to the left shoulder. Wrap the yarn smoothly from the underarm to the hip until previous work is covered smoothly. Repeat wraps, if necessary, to cover the body.

   †The yarn color will be specified in the pattern. If no specific color is given, use MC. If done in a color other than the body color, this will create a shirt, blouse, or bodice.

- Create the hips/bloomers by wrapping the yarn directly from the skein† in a figure-8 pattern. Work *from the front of the right upper hip, around the back of the right hip, between the legs to the left front hip, around the back of the left hip, and between the legs to the front right hip. Repeat from *, building up the yarn in successive wraps, starting at the hips and ending at the upper thigh, until the hip area is neatly covered and the shape is pleasing. You must build hips for the female characters, or the skirts will not stay up. Anchor and snip.

   †The yarn color will be specified in the pattern. If no specific color is given, use MC. If done in a color other than the body color, this will create bloomers.

HAIR

Basic Wig

- Wrap the hair-color yarn 120 times around a 9in/23cm board. Cut the yarn from the skein. Fold a 40in/102cm piece of hair yarn in half and secure the first bundle of 12 strands with a lark's head knot at the center point of the board. Continue to tie fringe by using a series of lark's head knots across the wraps, making ten bunches of 12 strands each. Cut the fringe open opposite the secured edge. Remove from the board. Fold the hair piece in half using a piece of paper to keep the fringe separate. Thread a tapestry needle with hair-color yarn and sew the center knots together, lacing from one to the next to close the center seam. Place the wig on the head and sew or knot on to secure. To provide better coverage at the front of the head of the female characters, smooth the hair and place a part where desired. Then, take the first 15 strands on each side of the face and gather them into a low ponytail at the back of the head, under the other hair. Secure with a constrictor knot using a 24in/61cm piece of hair-color yarn.

- For hair that is knotted on with lark's head knots to the head, a crochet hook is optional, but helpful.

FACE

- If the pattern indicates an eye color, the eye is embroidered in the manner of the eye diagram chart (see page 39). See the chart on page 38 for the number of strands of embroidery floss to use.

- Thread a tapestry needle with embroidery floss to make small straight stitches or knots for the mouth and brows. Lashes are made with a doubled three-strand piece of embroidery floss, knotted on the eye. Clip to about ½in/1.25cm. Dampen the floss and comb the strands with the tip of a needle to separate the lashes.

- Thread a tapestry needle with a piece of body-color yarn. Anchor the yarn at one side of the head and wrap it the indicated number of times around three strands at the side of the head to make an ear. Bring the needle up at the center front of the face and make a stitch around the center three strands of the face for the nose. Bring the needle up at the other side of the face and wrap the yarn the indicated number of times around three strands to make the other ear.

- Rub blush on cheeks.

- After stitching or knotting on features, anchor and snip all loose ends of floss to secure and hide.

EMBROIDERY FLOSS AMOUNTS

ADULT

Pupil (and lashes): 12 strands black (six doubled)

Iris: Six strands color (three doubled)

Eye Highlight: Eight strands white floss (four doubled)

Mouth: Six strands lip color (three doubled)

Eyebrows: Four strands (two doubled)

Ears: Five horizontal wraps of yarn over three strands of face yarn, then three vertical wraps encasing the original five wraps.

PRETEEN (James and Louise)

Pupil (and lashes): Ten strands black (five doubled)

Iris: Six strands color (three doubled)

Eye Highlight: Six strands white floss (three doubled)

Mouth: Six strands lip color (three doubled)

Eyebrows: Four strands (two doubled)

Ears: Five horizontal wraps of yarn over three strands of face yarn, then three vertical wraps encasing the original five wraps.

CHILDREN (George, Isla, Savannah, and Mia)

Pupil (and lashes): Eight strands black (four doubled)

Iris: Six strands color (three doubled)

Eye Highlight: Four strands white floss (two doubled)

Mouth: Six strands lip color (three doubled)

Eyebrows: Two strands (one doubled)

Ears: Four horizontal wraps of yarn over three strands of face yarn, then two vertical wraps encasing the original four wraps.

BABY (Charlotte)

Eyes are a French knot of doubled six-strand floss, surrounded by a lazy daisy stitch of blue six-strand floss. Lashes are six strands knotted on. The white is two strands doubled to make a small straight stitch. The mouth is two straight stitches made of one strand doubled of light peachy pink floss. Ears are four horizontal wraps of yarn over three strands of face yarn, then two vertical wraps encasing the original four wraps.

NOTE: The eyes for preteens and children are embroidered in the same manner as the eyes for adults, using the indicated amount of strands of floss.

DIAGRAM FOR ADULT LEFT EYE

(Reverse shaping for right eye)

NOTE: Each strand of facial yarn is labeled with a number that coordinates to its left or right edge.

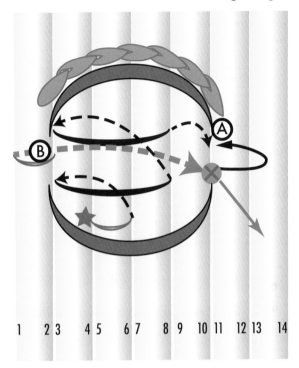

PUPIL

Thread tapestry needle with 36 inches of six-strand black embroidery floss. The pupil, outer eye, and eyelashes are all made from this same thread.

Double and knot at bottom to secure (12 strands). Anchor knot in back of doll's head and come up at starting point. [★]. Bring thread across strand of facial yarn and down at (6). Go behind two strands of yarn and come up at (3). Make a straight stitch from (3) to (8).*

Slide the needle behind three strands of facial yarn, exit at (3), and make another straight stitch from (3) to (8).* Repeat from * as desired for coverage. Slide the needle behind one strand of yarn and exit at (10).

COMMENCE OUTER EYE LAZY DAISY STITCH

Commence at starting point (A) and work in a counterclockwise direction. Anchor Lazy Daisy Stitch over one strand of facial yarn at the inner corner of the eye (B), and end the stitch by sliding the needle under the facial yarn, and then exit the needle at (A).

CREATE KNOT FOR THE EYELASHES

Cut floss and remove the needle, leaving 6-inch tails. Divide tails into two equal bunches of strands. Thread needle with one bunch and insert needle at (12). Go behind the strand of facial yarn and exit the needle at (11). Remove the needle and knot the two bunches together to secure. Fan out the strands and trim the lashes.

COLORED PART OF THE EYE (IRIS)

Embroider split stitches using floss in the iris color, along the top part of the eye stitches.

HIGHLIGHT

Using white floss, embroider a straight stitch highlight in the inner corner of the right eye and the outer corner of the left eye.

TIPS

* Use yarn that is unwound from the outside of the skein for the head and body, because it will yield smoother pieces of yarn.

* Use the constrictor knot to make a tight knot.

* Always secure new yarn by knotting it on somewhere inconspicuous. End work by anchoring and snipping yarn.

* Note that differing weights of yarn will change the proportions of the finished doll. Thus, a doll made from a DK weight yarn will be slimmer than a doll made from a heavy worsted-weight yarn.

* If a yarn is not strong enough to wrap tightly, wrap the figure with a stronger yarn first and then put a layer of the more fragile yarn on top.

* All of the dolls are made using the same basic directions. The different number of wraps and the size of the boards are specified in each individual pattern.

* Gauge is not important, so it is easy to substitute yarns.

* Make sure the back of the doll is covered as evenly as the front.

* Use the eye of a large tapestry needle to smooth strands into place.

* Hide all loose ends under wraps as you work.

* If you want to smooth the yarn used for a fringed hairpiece or skirt, iron it! I iron the fringe, combed out carefully, following the manufacturer's directions for the yarn, and I use a press cloth over the yarn to be safe. Remember, you want to smooth the yarn, not flatten it entirely!

* Facial features can be embroidered, painted, or attached as desired.

* For best results, make sure to wrap legs very firmly.

The Patterns

Queen Elizabeth II's Coronation—June 2, 1953

FINISHED HEIGHT 11in/28cm

MATERIALS

Yarn

- Lion Brand® Vanna's Choice® 3.5oz/100g, 170yds/156m (100% acrylic)—one skein each: #860-123 Beige (MC), #860-126 Chocolate (A), #860-145 Eggplant (B)

- Lion Brand® Wool-Ease® 3oz/85g, 197yds/180m (80% acrylic, 20% wool)—one skein: #620-129B Cocoa (C)

- Lion Brand® Vanna's Glamour® 1.75oz/50g, 202yds/185m (96% acrylic, 4% metallic polyester)—one skein each: #861-100 Diamond (D), #861-171 Gold (E)

- Lion Brand® Homespun® 6oz/170g, 185yds/169m (98% acrylic, 2% polyester)—one skein: #790-300 Hepplewhite (F)

- Anchor Artiste Metallic .88 oz/25g, 109yds/100m (80% viscose, 20% metalized polyester)—one ball: #302 (G). This yarn will be worked with two strands held together. One strand of a heavier metallic thread could be used.

- Lion Brand® Glitterspun® 16ft/5m (80% polyester, 20% nylon)—one card: #605-109 Sapphire (H)

Other Tools

- Sharp scissors, a ruler, stiff cardboard, and a large, blunt-tipped tapestry needle

- Six-strand embroidery floss in black, white, brown, blue, and rose pink

- Powder blush or paint for cheeks

- Metallic floss

- Size 7 (4.5mm) crochet hook [to crochet crown]

- Medium tip permanent marker in black

DOLL

Follow the basic directions for the Large Doll using MC.

Shoes: Use E.

Legs/Tights: Use MC.

Shirt/Upper Body: Use D. Wrap the body following the basic directions for the Large Doll, repeating the wraps as needed for coverage. Cover with a few wraps at the top of each arm, creating short sleeves. Using E, wrap a few times at the bottom of each sleeve for sleeve trim. Anchor and snip.

Skirt: Cut 120 pieces of D, 18in/46cm long. Make a lark's head knot fringe of 40 three-strand knots over a doubled 36in/92cm piece of D. Tie the fringe around the waist firmly, and trim the skirt to the desired length. Cut a 72in/183cm piece of E. Double the yarn, so you have a piece that is 36in/92cm long. † Twist this piece until it doubles back upon itself to make cording. Wrap a few wraps of E around the waist. Decorate the top of the skirt with loops of the cording. Secure the loops with stitches at the top of the waist wraps, or they can be looped over the waist wraps as well. Cover the top of the waist with more wraps of E for a sash.

Bloomers: Use D.

Cape: Cut 45 pieces of B and 12 pieces of F, 24in/61cm long. Make a lark's head knot fringe over a doubled 24in/61cm piece of F. Each knot is made up of three pieces of yarn. Make the fringe in this sequence: three two-strand knots of F, 15 three-strand knots of B, and three two-strand knots of F. Push the knots together firmly to create a dense fringe. Thread **one** end of the foundation thread into a tapestry needle and secure to one shoulder. Repeat for the other shoulder. Make two 6in/15cm cords from 12in/30.5cm pieces as above (see †) of metallic floss. Knot and trim both ends of each cord, and attach one to each shoulder. Dot the white part of the cape with the permanent marker to create the effect of ermine. Trim cape.

Hair: Wrap one strand each of A and C held together 40 times around a 9in/23cm board. Make a wig following the basic directions for the Large Doll. Sew the wig to the doll. Cut 15 pieces each of A and C 18in/46cm long. Make a series of lark's head knots around the hairline, using one strand of each color held together. Roll the front of the hair back to create the hairstyle. Secure with a few stitches if desired. Gather the rest of the hair into a low ponytail, and tie in place with a piece of yarn. Trim hair ends.

Face: Follow the basic directions for the Large Doll, using blue floss to embroider the colored part of the eye and brown floss for the brows.

CORONATION CROWN

Finished Height: 3in/7.5cm to top of bobble

Under Part

Using size 7 (4.5mm) hook and F, ch 33. Join with a sl st in first ch to form a ring. Turn.

Rnd 1: Ch 1, sc in each ch, sl st in first sc to join—32 sts.

Rnd 2: Switch to B. Ch 1, sc in back loop of each sc, sl st in first sc to join—32 sts. (*)

Rnds 3–10: Ch 1, sc in each sc, sl st in first sc to join—32 sts.

Rnd 11 (decrease): Ch 1, (sc in next 2 sc, sc2tog) 8 times, sl st in first sc to join—24 sts.

Rnd 12: Ch 1, sc in each sc, sl st in first sc to join—24 sts.

Rnd 13 (decrease): Ch 1, (sc in next 2 sc, sc2tog) 6 times, sl st in first sc to join—18 sts.

Rnd 14 (decrease): Ch 1, (sc in next sc, sc2tog) 6 times, sl st in first sc to join—12 sts.

Rnd 15 (decrease): Ch 1, (sc2tog) 6 times, sl st in first sc to join—6 sts.

Fasten off, leaving a tail. Thread the tail through the tapestry needle and run it through the remaining six stitches; draw up tightly to close the space at the top of the hat. Weave in the ends.

Metallic Part (Use two strands of G held together as one)

Holding crown bottom up, attach B to first free loop at beg of Rnd 2 (*). Ch 1, sc in front loop of each sc of Rnd 2, join with sl st in first sc to join—32 sts.

Rnd 1: Ch 1, *sc in next sc, [sc, dc, ch 3, (sc and hdc) in 3rd ch from hook] all in next sc, (dc and sc) in next sc, sc in next sc—small point made, (sc, hdc, dc) in next sc, (dc, trc, ch 3, sc and hdc in 3rd ch from hook) all in next sc, (trc and dc) in next sc, (dc, hdc, sc) in next sc—large point made. Rep from * 4 times, sl st in first sc to join—4 small points and 4 large points made. Fasten off. Fold points up against under part of crown.

Attach A to the top of the first small point (point #1). Ch 25, and sl st in the top of the small point on the other side of the crown (point #3). End off. Attach A to small point #2, ch 25, and sl st in the top of the small point on the other side of the crown (point #4). Fasten off. Weave in all ends.

Top Bobble

With A, ch 2, *wrap the yarn around the hook and draw up a loop in the first ch, rep from * until there are nine loops on the hook. Wrap the yarn around the hook, and draw through all nine loops. Ch 1, fasten off, leaving a tail to sew down. Sew the bobble to the top of the crown, securing the chains down at the same time.

FINISHING

Use the marker to dot black spots on Rnd 1 to create an "ermine" effect. Thread the tapestry needle with H and make a "jewel" of four straight stitches at the top of each large point. Weave in all ends.

Prince Philip, Duke of Edinburgh

FINISHED HEIGHT 11in/28cm

MATERIALS

Yarn

- Debbie Bliss™ Cashmerino Aran 1.75oz/50g, 98yds/90m (55% merino wool/33% acrylic/12% cashmere)—one skein each: #79 Nude (MC), #28 Charcoal (A), #25 White (B)†, #04 Navy (C)

- Small amounts of black, medium blue, and gray yarn

  † To make Prince Philip as a young man, as on Queen Elizabeth II's Coronation Day on June 2, 1953 [see page 4], substitute for hair, Color White (B): Debbie Bliss™ Rialto DK 1.75oz/50g, 115 yds/105m (100% extra fine merino wool)—one skein: #67 Camel (B)

Other Tools

- Sharp scissors, a ruler, stiff cardboard, and a large, blunt-tipped tapestry needle

- Six-strand embroidery floss in black, white, blue, red, green, yellow, light gray, rose pink, and metallic silver

- Powder blush or paint for cheeks

- Crochet hook (3mm, or correct size to use with metallic floss for Maltese Cross)

DOLL

Follow the basic directions for the Large Doll using MC.

Shoes: Use black yarn.

Legs/Trousers: Use A. Wrap four layers, building up the layers at the bottom to form pant cuffs. Wrap as for bloomers to create the hips.

Arm Bundle (Make 1): Use MC and 45 wraps. Wrap ½in/1cm at the wrists in B. Wrap the rest of the arm bundle in C for the jacket sleeves.

Shirt/Vest/Jacket: With B, wrap to cover the chest for the shirt, anchor and snip. Switch to medium blue yarn, and wrap from the right shoulder to the crotch, then over the left shoulder a few times to create the vest. Anchor and snip. Switch to C, and wrap around the upper arms, building up layers of wraps, following the basic directions sequence to create a jacket. Build layers of wraps around the shoulders and upper arms, then wrap two layers down the arms to build sleeves. Wrap around the hips to create a tuxedo. End with a few wraps at the waist to cinch in the center. Wrap medium blue yarn around the waist to create a cummerbund. Wrap a piece of B around the neck 12 times to create a collar. Cut three 12in/30.5cm pieces of gray yarn and wrap around the white collar once, then tie in an overhand knot at the front to create a necktie. Trim and tuck ends under vest to secure.

Medals: Cut 12 8in/20cm pieces of different color embroidery flosses. Using one piece of floss as the foundation, make a lark's head knot fringe with 11 pieces of colored floss. Sew the fringe to the uniform, and trim evenly so that the fringe resembles the ribbons that hold medals. A little water will tame the floss and make it easier to cut in a straight line.

Hair: Follow the basic directions for the Large Doll, using B, wrapping 77 times around a 7in/18cm board. Knot 11 bunches of seven strands. Sew the wig to the doll. Cut 40 6in/15cm pieces of yarn and make two-strand lark's head knots around the hairline, in front of the wig. Trim all hair.

Face: Follow the basic directions for the Large Doll, using blue floss to embroider the colored part of the eye. Use four strands of light gray floss to make straight stitch eyebrows.

ORDER OF MERIT CROSS NECKLACE

Cut one 12in/30.5cm piece each of red and blue floss for neck ribbon.

Using metallic floss and crochet hook, ch 6 (foundation chain), sc in second ch from hook and in next ch, (ch 3, sc in second ch from hook and in next ch), sc in next ch of foundation ch, (ch 3, sc in second ch from hook and in next ch), 2 sc in each of last 2 ch sts of foundation chain. Fasten off leaving an 8in/20cm tail. Thread the tail through a tapestry needle, then wrap the tail around the center of the cross in a crisscross fashion. Secure the end of the tail through the back of the cross. Attach the cross to the neck ribbon by making a few overhand stitches around the neck ribbon. Fasten off. Tie the necklace around the neck, trim the ends.

Queen Elizabeth II on Her 90th Birthday

FINISHED HEIGHT 10½in/26.5cm
MATERIALS

Yarn

- Cascade Yarns® 220 Superwash® 3.5oz/100g, 220yds/200m (100% superwash wool)—one skein each: #228 Frosted Almond (MC), #815 Black (A), #871 White (B), #850 Lime Sherbert (C) [to crochet hat only]

- Cascade Yarns® 220 Superwash® Effects 3.5oz/100g, 220yds/200m (100% superwash merino wool)—one skein: #07 Daffodil (D)

- Small amounts of yellow, white, and dark green yarn [to make flower for hat]

Other Tools

- Sharp scissors, a ruler, stiff cardboard, and a large, blunt-tipped tapestry needle

- Six-strand embroidery floss in black, white, blue, light gray, rose pink, and metallic gold

- Powder blush or paint for cheeks

- Size G-6 (4mm) crochet hook [to crochet hat]

DOLL

Follow the basic directions for the Large Doll using MC.

Head/Body/Leg Bundle (Make 2): Use MC and 80 wraps. Wrap each leg with two layers to add a little bulk to the ankles and legs.

Shoes: Use A.

Legs/Tights: Use MC.

Arm Bundle (Make 1): Use B and 60 wraps. Make hands as in the basic directions for the Large Doll and wrap from the wrist up the arms for 1in/2.5cm to create gloves. Wrap the rest of the arm bundle in D for jacket sleeves.

Shirt/Upper Body/Bloomers: Wrap using D. Continue to wrap in the established pattern until the body is covered and has a full shape. Wrap a double layer of yarn to create the sleeves, and wrap a few extra layers to form cuffs. Thread a tapestry needle with metallic floss and create a brooch on the front of the chest by making a series of stitches overlap in a star shape.

Skirt: Cut 81 pieces of D, 18in/46cm long. Make a lark's head knot fringe over a doubled 24in/61cm piece of D. Each knot is made up of three strands of yarn. Trim the fringe to 4in/10cm. Tie the skirt around the waist. Wrap yarn around the waist for a sash.

Hair: Cut 44 12in/30.5cm pieces of B. Make 22 lark's head knots, each using two strands of yarn, around the hairline. Wrap B 60 times around a 6in/15cm board. Make a wig, following the basic directions for the Large Doll, and attach the wig to the head behind the knots at the hairline. Roll the hair to approximate the Queen's hairstyle, and use a few stitches to secure the rolls.

Face: Follow the basic directions for the Large Doll, using blue floss to embroider the colored part of the eye and gray floss for the brows.

HAT

Finished Height: 2½in/6cm

Rnd 1: Using C, wind the yarn around two fingers to make a loop (Magic Ring). Ch 1, 6 sc in loop, tighten loop, sl st in first ch 1 to join—6 sts.

Rnd 2: Ch 1, (sc in next sc, 2 sc in next sc) 3 times, sl st in first ch 1 to join—9 sts.

Rnd 3: Ch 1, (2 sc in next sc) 9 times, sl st in first ch 1 to join —18 sts.

Rnd 4: Ch 1, (sc in next 2 sc, 2 sc in next sc) 6 times, sl st in first ch 1 to join—24 sts.

Rnd 5: Ch 1, (sc in next 3 sc, 2 sc in next sc) 6 times, sl st in first ch 1 to join—30 sts.

Rnd 6: Ch 1, (sc in next 4 sc, 2 sc in next sc) 6 times, sl st in first ch 1 to join—36 sts.

Rnd 7: Ch 1, (sc in next 5 sc, 2 sc in next sc) 6 times, sl st in first ch 1 to join—42 sts.

Rnd 8: Ch 1, (sc in next 6 sc, 2 sc in next sc) 6 times, sl st in first ch 1 to join—48 sts.

Rnd 9: Ch 1, (sc in next 5 sc, 2 sc in next sc) 8 times, sl st in first ch 1 to join—56 sts.

Rnd 10: Ch 1, sc in back loop of each sc, sl st in first ch 1 to join—56 sts.

Rnds 11–13: Ch 1, sc in each sc, sl st in first ch 1 to join—56 sts.

Rnd 14: Ch 1, (sc in next 5 sc, sc2 tog) 8 times, sl st into first ch 1 to join—48 sts.

Rnds 15–16: Ch 1, sc in each sc, sl st into first ch 1 to join—48 sts.

Rnd 17: Ch 1, (sc in next 6 sc, sc2 tog) 6 times, sl st into first ch 1 to join—42 sts.

Rnds 18–21: Ch 1, sc in each sc, sl st into first ch 1 to join—42 sts.

Rnd 22: Ch 1, sc in back loop of each sc, sl st into first ch 1 to join—42 sts.

Brim

Rnd 1: Ch 1, sc in next 4 sc, 2 sc in each of next 2 sc, (sc in next 5 sc, 2 sc in next sc) 6 times, sl st in first sc to join—50 sts.

Rnd 2: Ch 1, (sc in next 4 sc, 2 sc in next sc) 10 times, sl st in first sc to join—60 sts.

Rnd 3: Ch 1, sc in each sc, sl st in first sc to join—60 sts.

Rnd 4: Ch 1, (sc in next 5 sc, 2 sc in next sc) 10 times, sl st in first sc to join—70 sts.

Rnd 5: Ch 1, sc in back loop of each sc, sl st in first sc to join—70 sts.

Fasten off.

Large White Flower (Make 2)

Using yellow yarn, wind the yarn around two fingers to make a loop (Magic Ring). Ch 1, 5 sc in loop, tighten loop, sl st into ch 1 to join—5 sts. Fasten off yarn.

Attach white yarn.

Next Rnd: [Sl st in next sc, ch 2, (dc, ch 2, sl st) in same sc] 5 times, sl st in first sl st to close rnd. Fasten off.

Yellow Flower

Using yellow yarn, wind the yarn around two fingers to make a loop (Magic Ring). Ch 1, 5 sc in loop, tighten loop, sl st in ch 1 to join—5 sts.

Next Rnd: Ch 1, (Sl st in next sc, ch3, work a sl st into first ch, sl st into same sc) 5 times, sl st in ch 1 to join. Fasten off.

Pair of Leaves

Using dark green yarn, ch 10, sl st in second ch from hook, (hdc and dc) in next ch, hdc in next ch, sc in next ch, sl st in next ch, sc in next ch, hdc in next ch, (dc and hdc) in next ch, sl st in last ch. Fasten off.

BONUS ACCESSORY TO CROCHET

HANDBAG

Finished Height: 2in/4.5cm, not including handles

Setup Rnd: Ch 11 with A. Work (2 sc, ch 1) in 2nd ch from hook for side, sc in 8 chs for front, (ch 1, 2 sc, ch 1) in next ch for side, working on opposite side of beginning ch, sc in back loop of 8 chs for back, ch 1, sl st in first sc to join.

Rnd 1: Ch 1, sc in back loop of 2 sc, ch 1, skip ch 1 from prev rnd, sc in the back loops of 8 sc, ch 1, skip ch 1 from prev rnd, sc in the back loop of 2 sc, ch 1, skip ch 1 from prev rnd, sc in the back loops of 8 sc, ch 1, skip ch 1 from prev rnd, sl st in the first sc to join.

Rnds 2–5: Ch 1, sc in 2 sc, ch 1, skip ch1 from prev rnd, sc in 8 sc, ch 1, skip ch1 from prev rnd, sc in 2 sc, skip ch 1 from prev rnd, ch 1, sc in 8 sc, ch 1, skip ch 1 from prev rnd, sl st in first sc to join—20 sts.

Rnd 6: Ch 1, sc2tog, ch 1, skip ch 1 from prev rnd, sc in 8 sc, ch 1, skip ch1 from prev rnd, sc2tog, skip ch 1 from prev rnd, ch 1, sc in 8 sc, ch 1, skip ch 1 from prev rnd, sl st in first sc to join—18 sts.

Rnds 7–8: Ch 1, sc in next sc, ch 1, skip ch 1 from prev rnd, sc in 8 sc, ch 1, skip ch 1 from prev rnd, sc in 1 sc, skip ch 1 from prev rnd, ch 1, sc in 8 sc, ch 1, skip ch 1 from prev rnd, sl st in first sc to join—18 sts. Fasten off.

Handles (Make 2): Ch 21 with A, 2 sc in second ch from hook, sl st in each of next 18 ch sts, (2 sc and sl st) in last ch. Fasten off.

FINISHING

Block lightly, weave in ends. Sew handles to bag.

QUEEN ELIZABETH II
and PRINCE PHILIP

Diana, Princess of Wales

FINISHED HEIGHT 11in/28cm

MATERIALS

Yarn

- Patons® Canadiana™ 3.5oz/100g, 205yds/187m (100% acrylic)—one skein each: #10010 Flax (MC), #10022 Oatmeal (A), #10610 Fools Gold (B)

- Patons® Metallic™ 3oz/85g, 252yds/230m (63% nylon/28% acrylic/9% wool)—one ball: #95042 Platinum (C)

- Patons® Silk Bamboo™ 2.2oz/65g, 102yds/93m (70% viscose from bamboo/30% silk)—one ball: #85008 Ivory (D)

- Patons® Glam Stripes™ 2.1oz/60g, 261yds/239m (90% acrylic/10% polyester)—one skein: #09005 White Silver (E)

- Patons® Lace Sequin™ 2.5oz/70g, 343yds/314m (68% acrylic/14% polyester/9% wool/9% mohair)—one skein: #37005 Crystal (F) [to crochet tiara and veil only]

- Small amount of white yarn

Other Tools

- Sharp scissors, a ruler, stiff cardboard, and a large, blunt-tipped tapestry needle

- Six-strand embroidery floss in black, light golden brown, white, blue, and rose pink

- Powder blush or paint for cheeks

- Size G-6 (4mm) crochet hook [to crochet tiara and veil]

DOLL

Follow the basic directions for the Large Doll using MC.

Shoes: Use C.

Legs: Use MC.

Arm Bundle (Make 1): Use MC and 45 wraps.

Upper Body/Bodice: Wrap the upper body following the basic directions for the Large Doll using D. Make rope trim for the neck flounce as follows. Cut a 6yd/5.5m piece of C. Fold it in half, then in half again (four strands). Twist firmly until the piece doubles back on itself; knot the ends so that it doesn't unravel. Thread a tapestry needle with an 18in/46cm piece of yarn. Anchor the yarn to the end of the rope. Create a zigzag from the rope with peaks that are ¾in/2cm. Stitch the top of two peaks together. Continue to stitch the tops together until you have enough of a collar to fit around a V neck and to reach around the back. Firmly stitch the rope ends together with an overhand stitch. Anchor and snip. Sew to the neckline.

Sleeves (Make 2): Cut 30 6in/15cm pieces of D. Make a lark's head knot fringe over a doubled 24in/61cm piece of D. You will be wrapping the next layer of yarn over the top of the fringe, so it will be easier to wrap smoothly if the shoulder is at the

top (north), and the wrist is at the bottom (south) as you wrap. Hold the fringe in place against the top of the arm. Switch to E and wrap the yarn, starting at the shoulder, covering the top of the fringe, until you are 1½in/4cm from the wrist. Wrap back up to the shoulder, then continue to wrap, building layers, until the shoulder measures 4in/10cm in circumference. Anchor and snip. Repeat for the other arm. Trim the fringe. Cut two 8in/20cm pieces of C. Wrap the yarn at the top of the fringe, and tie a bow. Repeat for the other sleeve.

Underskirt: Cut 80 18in/46cm pieces of A. Make a two-strand lark's head knot fringe over a doubled 36in/92cm piece of A. Tie it around the waist at the hips. Trim to desired length.

Gown Skirt: Cut 96 18in/46 cm pieces of D, and 16 pieces of E. Make a lark's head knot fringe over a doubled 36in/92cm piece of A in this sequence: 16 knots of D (three strands each), four knots of E (four strands each), 16 knots of D (three strands each). Tie the fringe around the waist at the hips on top of the underskirt. Trim to desired length.

Hair: Follow the basic directions for the Large Doll, using B. Roll the front of the hair back, and secure with a few stitches if desired. Trim the hair.

Face: Follow the basic directions for the Large Doll, using blue floss to embroider the colored part of the eye and light golden brown for the brows.

TIARA AND VEIL

Stitch Glossary

MB: Make bobble. Yo, insert hook from front to back of next st as if to make a dc, pull through one loop, (yo, insert hook in same st from front to back, pull through loop) three times, yo and pull through all nine loops on hook. Bobble made.

Tiara

Using C, ch 42. Sl st in first ch to make a ring.

Rnd 1: Ch 1, sc in each ch, sl st into beginning ch1 to join—41 sts.

Rnd 2: Sl st in each of first 10 sc, [(sc and hdc) in next sc, work (dc, MB, ch 2, sc in second ch from hook, dc) in next sc, (hdc and sc) in next sc] 7 times, sl st in each of next 10 sc, sl st into first sl st to join. Fasten off, weave in ends.

Veil

Cut about 30 36in/92cm pieces of F and make a lark's head knot fringe with single strand knots over a doubled piece of 18in/46 cm piece of white yarn.

FINISHING

Sew the veil to the inside of the tiara. Trim veil ends.

Prince Charles, Prince of Wales

MATERIALS

FINISHED HEIGHT 10¾in/27cm

Yarn

- Lion Brand® Vanna's Choice® 3.5oz/100g, 170yds/156m (100 % acrylic)—one skein each: #860-123 Beige (MC,) #860-153 Black (A), #860-110 Navy (B), #860-100 White (C), # 860-405 Silver Heather (D)

- Small amounts of white, gold, metallic gold, and medium blue yarn

Other Tools

- Sharp scissors, a ruler, stiff cardboard, and a large, blunt-tipped tapestry needle

- Six-strand embroidery floss in black, gray, white, green, and rose pink

- For ribbons: small amounts of red, white, purple, and blue embroidery floss

- Powder blush or paint for cheeks

DOLL

Follow the basic directions for the Large Doll using MC, and refer to photo of Prince Charles on **page 10.**

Shoes: Use color A.

Legs/Trousers: Use color B. Wrap three layers, building up the layers at the bottom to form pant cuffs. Wrap as for bloomers to create the hips.

Arm Bundle (Make 1): Use MC. Make the hand with MC; wrap the rest of the arm bundle with B for jacket sleeves.

Jacket/Upper Body: Use B, building up layers of wraps, following the basic directions sequence to create a jacket. Build layers of wraps around the shoulders and upper arms, then wrap two layers down the arms to build sleeves. Wrap around the hips to create a longer jacket. Wrap gold yarn around the neck ten times, then wrap white yarn over the gold to create a collar. Thread a tapestry needle with gold yarn and knot or embroider French knots for buttons. Wrap medium blue yarn from the shoulder to the hip ten times to create a sash. Thread a tapestry needle with gold yarn.

Wrapping around the existing wraps, wrap or stitch the gold yarn three times at the top of each shoulder from the neck to the top of the arm to create epaulets. Wrap gold yarn around the waist for a belt. Anchor and snip all yarn ends.

Trim: Cut three 36in/92cm pieces of metallic gold yarn. Knot the strands together and twist the yarn until it doubles back upon itself to create rope trim. Knot at the ends and wrap around the arm and under the epaulet. Tie on or stitch to secure. Cut eight 8in/20cm pieces of different color embroidery flosses. Using one piece of floss as the foundation, make a lark's head knot fringe with seven pieces of colored floss. Sew the fringe to the uniform, and trim evenly so that the fringe resembles the ribbons that hold medals. A little water will tame the floss and make it easier to cut in a straight line.

Hair: Cut 65 8in/20cm pieces each of C and D. Holding one strand of each color together, make lark's head knots around the circumference of the head to form a hairline, then fill in with concentric circles of knots until the head is evenly covered. Cut a few 8in/20cm pieces of white and add a few lark's head knots at the front as in the photograph.

Face: Follow the basic directions for the Large Doll, using blue floss to embroider the colored part of the eye and gray floss for the brows.

Camilla, Duchess of Cornwall

FINISHED HEIGHT 11in/28cm

MATERIALS

Yarn

- Lion Brand® Vanna's Choice® 3.5oz/100g, 170yds/156m (100 % acrylic)—one skein each: #860-123 Beige (MC), #860-105 Silver Blue (A), #860-099 Linen (B)

- Lion Brand® Vanna's Glamour® 1.75oz/50g, 202yds/185m (96% polyester/4% metallic polyester)—one skein: #861-100 Diamond (C)

- Martha Stewart Crafts™/MC Glitter Ribbon 1¾oz/50g, 69yds/63m (62% polyester/38% metallic polyester)—one ball: #5900-506 Blue Sapphire (D)

- Lion Brand® Baby Soft® 5oz/140g, 459yds/420m (60% acrylic/40% polyamid)—one skein: #920-157 Pale Yellow (E)

- Small amounts of gray yarn

Other Tools

- Sharp scissors, a ruler, stiff cardboard, and a large, blunt-tipped tapestry needle

- Six-strand embroidery floss in black, light golden brown, blue, white, and rose pink

- Powder blush or paint for cheeks

DOLL

Follow the basic directions for the Large Doll using MC.

Shoes: Use gray yarn.

Legs/Bloomers: Use MC for the legs and A for the bloomers.

Shirt/Upper Body: Wrap body using C, repeating the sequence as needed for coverage, then switch to color A and wrap the arms from the shoulder to the wrist, then back up to the shoulders. Wrap D around the shoulders in a figure-8 pattern across the back to create the trim at the shoulder edge. Anchor and snip.

Skirt: Cut 12in/30.5cm pieces of yarn: four D, 48 A, and 28 C. Make a lark's head knot fringe over a 24in/61cm doubled piece of B. The sequence is

12 knots A (two strands), one knot D (two strands), seven knots C (four strands), one knot D (two strands), and 12 knots A (two strands). Trim the fringe evenly and tie it around the waist. Tie a 24in/61cm piece of D at the waist for a sash.

Hair: Follow the basic directions for the Large Doll, using a combination of B and E. Wrap one strand of B 60 times, and one strand of E 120 times. Knot the hair into 18 bundles of ten strands. Attach the wig to the head. Roll some front pieces of hair back for the hairstyle and secure with a few stitches. Trim the remaining pieces of hair.

Face: Follow the basic directions for the Large Doll, using blue floss to embroider the colored part of the eye and light golden brown floss for the brows.

Princess Anne, Princess Royal

FINISHED HEIGHT 10¾in/27cm

MATERIALS

Yarn

- Debbie Bliss® Cashmerino Aran 1.75oz/50g, 98yds/90m (55% wool/33% acrylic/12% cashmere)—one skein each: #79 Nude (MC), #04 Navy (A), #65 Bark (B), #25 White (C), #300 Black (D) [(C) to crochet hat only]

- Small amounts of black, gold, red, light blue, white, and yellow yarn

Other Tools

- Sharp scissors, a ruler, stiff cardboard, and a large, blunt-tipped tapestry needle

- Six-strand embroidery floss in black, white, blue, medium brown, metallic gold, and rose pink

- For ribbons: Six-strand embroidery floss in red, light green, yellow, light blue, and white

- Powder blush or paint for cheeks

- Size 7 (4.5mm) crochet hook [to crochet hat]

DOLL

Follow the basic directions for the Large Doll.

Head/Body/Leg Bundle (Make 2): Use MC and 75 wraps. Wrap the legs and bloomers in MC.

Shoes: Use D. Anchor and snip all yarn ends.

Arm Bundle (Make 1): Use MC and 55 wraps. Make the hands, then wrap the rest of the arm bundle in A for jacket sleeves. Wrap a thick stripe of gold yarn, bordered at the top and bottom with a thin stripe of red yarn at the wrist of each sleeve.

Shirt/Upper Body: Use A, building wraps to create a jacket. Wrap white yarn around the neck to create a collar. Anchor and snip all yarn ends. Wrap light blue yarn 12 times from the hip to the shoulder to create the sash.

Skirt: Cut 55 9in/23cm pieces of A. Make a lark's head knot fringe over a doubled 36in/92cm piece of A. Tie the skirt around the waist, and trim to make the hem even.

Trim: Cut seven 8in/20cm pieces of ribbon-color embroidery flosses. Using one piece of floss as the foundation, make a lark's head knot fringe with seven pieces of colored floss. Sew the fringe to the uniform, and trim evenly so that the fringe resembles the ribbons that hold medals. A little water will tame the floss and make it easier to cut in a straight line. Twist a doubled 36in/92cm piece of metallic floss until it doubles back on itself to create a cord. Fold the cord in half and secure it to the shoulder as shown. Knot the bottom of each end and trim.

Hair: Using B, make a basic wig as in the directions for the Large Doll, wrapping the yarn 120 times around a 9in/23cm board. Attach the wig to the head and roll back the front pieces of hair to create pronounced rolls on each side of the head. Make a low ponytail tied with a piece of yarn.

Face: Follow the basic directions for the Large Doll, using blue floss to embroider the colored part of the eye and medium brown floss for the brows.

BONUS ACCESSORY TO CROCHET

MILITARY HAT

Finished Height: 1½in/4cm

Crown

Rnd 1: Using C, wind the yarn around two fingers to make a loop (Magic Ring). Ch 1, 6 sc in loop, tighten loop sl st in ch1 to join—6 sts.

Rnd 2: Ch 1, (2 sc in next sc) 6 times, sl st in first ch 1 to join—12 sts.

Rnd 3: Ch 1, (sc in next sc, 2 sc in next sc) 6 times, sl st in first ch 1 to join—18 sts.

Rnd 4: Ch 1, (sc in next 2 sc, 2sc in next sc) 6 times, sl st in first ch 1 to join—24 sts.

Rnd 5: Ch 1, sc in each sc, sl st into first ch 1 to join—24 sts.

Rnd 6: Ch 1, (sc in next 2 sc, 2 sc in next sc) 8 times, sl st in first ch 1 to join—32 sts.

Rnd 7: Ch 1, sc in each sc, sl st in first ch 1 to join—32 sts.

Rnd 8: Ch 1, (sc in next 3 sc, 2 sc in next sc) 8 times, sl st in first ch 1 to join—40 sts.

Rnd 9: Ch 1, sc in back loop of each sc, sl st in first ch 1 to join—40 sts.

Rnds 10–11: Ch 1, sc in each sc, sl st in first ch 1 to join—40 sts.

Switch to yellow yarn.

Rnd 12: Ch 1, sc in each sc, sl st in first ch 1 to join—40 sts.

Switch to D.

Rnds 13–15: Ch 1, sc in each sc, sl st in first ch 1 to join—40 sts.

Brim

Rnd 1: Ch 1, sc in front loop of each sc to create beg of brim, sl st in first ch 1 to join—40 sts.

Rnd 2: Ch 1, (sc in next 4 sc, 2 sc in next sc) 8 times, sl st in first sc to join—48 sts.

Rnd 3: Ch 1, (sc in next 5 sc, 2 sc in next sc) 8 times, sl st in first sc to join—56 sts.

Rnd 4: Ch 1, sc in each sc, sl st in first sc to join—56 sts.

Rnd 5: Ch 1, turn work. With the wrong side of the brim facing, sl st in each sc. Fasten off.

FINISHING

Thread a tapestry needle with metallic floss and embroider three straight stitches in a "V" shape, secured at the bottom by a horizontal stitch for the emblem on the front of the hat. Weave in all ends.

Prince Andrew, Duke of York

FINISHED HEIGHT 10¾in/27cm

MATERIALS

Yarn

- Rowan Pure Wool Superwash DK 1.75oz/50g, 137yds/125m (100% wool)— two skeins each: #101 Chalk (MC), #110 Dust (A)

- Rowan Pure Wool Superwash Worsted 3.5 oz/50g, 200yds/219m, (100% wool)— one skein: #109 Black (B)

- Small amounts of teal blue, gold, gray, and white yarn

Other Tools

- Sharp scissors, a ruler, stiff cardboard, and a large, blunt-tipped tapestry needle

- Six-strand embroidery floss in black, metallic gold, white, grayish brown, blue, and rose pink

- For ribbons: Six-strand embroidery floss in light blue, yellow, red, and white

- Powder blush or paint for cheeks

DOLL

Follow the basic directions for the Large Doll using MC.

Head/Body/Leg Bundle (Make 2): Wrap MC 85 times around a 12in/30.5cm board. Wrap a yarn ball that is 8in/20cm in circumference to stuff the head.

Shoes: Use B to wrap for 1in/2.5cm on each side of the constrictor knot. Fold at the ankle and follow the directions for the Large Doll to finish the shoe.

Trousers: Use B. Wrap the legs for 4½in/11.5cm for three layers, building up wraps at the ankle to create the effect of trousers. Wrap as for bloomers to create hips. Anchor and snip.

Arm Bundle (Make 1): Wrap MC 65 times around a 9in/23cm board. Cover the arms with two layers of wraps of B for the sleeves.

Jacket: Use B to build up layers of wraps, following the basic directions sequence to create a jacket. Build layers of wraps around the shoulders and upper arms, and then wrap two layers down the arms to build the sleeves. Wrap around the hips to create a longer jacket. Wrap gold yarn around the neck ten times, then wrap white yarn over the gold to create a collar. Wrap teal blue yarn from the shoulder to the hip ten times to create a sash. Thread a tapestry needle with gold yarn. Stitch or wrap three straight stitches at each shoulder to create epaulets. Wrap gold yarn at the wrists to build up cuffs, and then wrap stripes of gold at the forearm. Thread a tapestry needle with metallic gold floss, and knot or embroider French knots for buttons. Wrap metallic gold floss around the waist several times for the belt. Anchor and snip all yarn ends. Make cord trim by cutting two 18in/46cm pieces of gold yarn or floss. Knot together and twist until the yarn doubles back on itself. Knot both ends to maintain the twist. Trim the ends. Thread the cord through an epaulet and knot or stitch down to secure.

Medals: Cut eight 8in/20cm pieces of different color embroidery floss. Using one piece of floss as the foundation, make a lark's head knot fringe with seven pieces of colored floss. Sew the fringe to the uniform, and trim it evenly so that the fringe resembles the ribbons that hold medals. A little water will tame the floss and make it easier to cut in a straight line.

Hair: Using A, cut 150 pieces, each 7in/18cm long. Using two pieces of yarn knotted over three strands of the face yarn, make a series of lark's head knots around the hairline, and then fill in the scalp with knots. Mix in some pieces of gray yarn with the A yarn around the hairline. Trim the hair.

Face: Follow the basic directions for the Large Doll, using blue floss to embroider the colored part of the eye and grayish brown floss for the brows.

Sarah Ferguson, Duchess of York

FINISHED HEIGHT 10¾in/27cm

MATERIALS

Yarn

- Red Heart® Super Saver™ 3.5oz/100g, 190yd/174m (100% acrylic)—one skein each: Either #E267-334 Tan *or* E300-334 Buff (MC), #300-312 Black (A), #E300-512 Turqua (B), #E300-256 Carrot (C)

Other Tools

- Sharp scissors, a ruler, stiff cardboard, and a large, blunt-tipped tapestry needle
- Six-strand embroidery floss in black, light rust brown, white, blue, and rose pink
- Powder blush or paint for cheeks
- H-8 (5mm) crochet hook [to crochet hat]

DOLL

Follow the basic directions for the Large Doll, using MC.

Shoes: Use A.

Legs: Use MC.

Dress Bodice/Upper Body: Wrap as in the basic directions for the Large Doll, using B. Wrap arms using MC and the upper arms using A to create sleeves.

Bloomers: Use B.

Skirt: Cut 60 14in/36cm pieces of B. Make a lark's head knot fringe of 30 two-strand knots over a doubled 36in/92cm piece of B. Trim the skirt to 3½in/9cm and tie it around the waist firmly.

Hair: Follow the basic directions for the Large Doll, using color C. Part the hair on the left. Make a braid on the left front side of the hair using nine strands. Wrap it to the back and secure.

Face: Follow the basic directions for the Large Doll, using blue floss to embroider the colored part of the eye and light rust brown floss for the brows.

HAT

Crown

Rnd 1: Using A, wind the yarn around two fingers to make a loop (Magic Ring). Ch 1, 6 sc in loop, tighten loop, sl st into first ch 1 to join—6 sts.

Rnd 2: Ch 1, (sc in next sc, 2 sc in next sc) 3 times, sl st in first ch 1 to join—9 sts.

Rnd 3: Ch 1, (2 sc in next sc) 9 times, sl st in first ch 1 to join—18 sts.

Rnd 4: Ch 1, (sc in next 2 sc, 2 sc in next sc) 6 times, sl st in first ch 1 to join—24 sts.

Rnd 5: Ch 1, (sc in next 3 sc, 2 sc in next sc) 6 times, sl st in first ch 1 to join—30 sts.

Rnd 6: Ch 1, sc in each sc, sl st in first ch 1 to join—30 sts.

Rnd 7: Ch 1, (sc in next 4 sc, 2 sc in next sc) 6 times, sl st in first ch 1 to join—36 sts.

Rnd 8: Ch 1, (sc in next 5 sc, 2 sc in next sc) 6 times, sl st in first ch 1 to join—42 sts.

Brim

Row 1 (RS): Ch 1, sc in back loop of next 18 sc, turn—18 sts.

Row 2 (WS): Ch 1, sc in 18 sc from the previous row, sc in front loop of next 2 sc of last rnd of crown, turn—20 sts.

Rnd 3: Ch 1, (sc in next 3 sc, 2 sc in next sc) 5 times, sc in back loop of next 2 sc of last rnd of crown; turn—27 sts.

Row 4: Ch 1, sc in 27 sc, sc in front loop of next 2 sc of crown, turn—29 sts.

Rnd 5: Ch 1, (sc in next 3 sc, 2 sc in next sc) 7 times, sc in next sc, sc in back loop of next 2 sc of crown, turn—38 sts.

Row 6: Ch 1, sc in 38 sc, sc in front loop of next 2 sc of crown, turn—40 sts.

Rnd 7: Ch 1, sc in next 3 sc, (sc in next 3 sc, 2 sc in next sc) 8 times, sc in next 5 sc, sc in back loop of next 2 sc of crown, turn—50 sts.

Row 8: Ch 1, sc in next 50 sc, sc in front loop of next 2 sc of crown, turn—52 sts.

Rnd 9: Ch 1, working all sts in back loops, sl st in next 18 sc, sc in next 6 sc, hdc in next 4 sc, sc in next 6 sc, sl st in next 8 sc, sl st in remaining crown stitches, sl st in first st to join. Fasten off.

Flourish

With B, ch 41.

Row 1: Sk 1st ch from hook, work (sc, hdc, dc, hdc) in each of next 7 chs, hdc in next 5 chs, sc in next 12 chs, sl st in next 16 chs. Fasten off. Coil the end into a flower shape and sew it down to the edge of the hat.

Princess Beatrice

FINISHED HEIGHT 11in/28cm

MATERIALS

- Rowan Baby Merino Silk DK 1.75oz/50g, 148yds/135m (66% wool, 34% silk)—two skeins: #690 Pebble (MC); one skein: #678 Rose (A)

- Rowan Pure Wool Superwash Worsted 3.5oz/100g, 219yds/200m (100% superwash wool)—one skein each: #111 Granite (B), #106 Rust (C)

- Rowan Felted Tweed 1.75oz/50g 175yds/191m (50% merino wool, 25% alpaca, 25% viscose)—one skein: #185 Frozen (D)

- Small amounts of black, white, dark gray, and metallic yarn†

† Anchor Artiste Metallic (distributed through the Rowan Yarn Company) .88oz/25g, 109yds/100m (80% viscose, 20% metalized polyester)—one ball: #302

Other Tools

- Sharp scissors, a ruler, stiff cardboard, and a large, blunt-tipped tapestry needle

- Six-strand embroidery floss in black, white, reddish brown, golden green, and rose pink

- Powder blush or paint for cheeks

- Size G-6 (4mm) crochet hook [to crochet hat]

DOLL

Head/Body/Leg Bundle (Make 2): Follow the basic directions for the Large Doll, wrapping MC 75 times around a 12in/30.5cm board. Use B to wrap the legs.

Shoes: Use black yarn.

Arm Bundle (Make 1): Use MC and 55 wraps. After the arm bundle is inserted into the body, wrap the upper arms lightly to create shoulders. Wrap the arms from shoulder to wrist with D to create sleeves. Wrap the cuffs with white yarn, and make the trim with one wrap of B at each wrist.

Bloomers: Use B.

Skirt: Cut 60 9in/23cm pieces of A. Make a lark's head fringe knot skirt of 20 knots of three strands each knotted over a doubled 24in/61cm piece of yarn.

Shirt/Upper Body: Wrap one layer of MC to create a smooth upper body. Switch to D, and wrap to create the jacket. Wrap in sequence as in the basic directions for the Large Doll. Tie the skirt around the waist. Then wrap D to cover the waistband and create the effect of a longer jacket. Switch to white yarn, and wrap ten times around the neck for a collar. Switch to B and wrap a few times at the base of the collar. Thread a tapestry needle with B yarn, and make a couple of long stitches/wraps down the front of the jacket for trim, and then three straight stitches for pockets. Anchor and snip. Embroider or knot on metallic thread buttons.

Hair: Using one strand of C, wrap yarn 120 times around a 9in/23cm board. Make a wig as in the basic directions for the Large Doll, making 12 bunches of ten strands each. Attach the wig to the head, and trim the hair.

Face: Follow the basic directions for the Large Doll, using golden green floss to embroider the colored part of the eye and reddish brown floss for the brows.

PILLBOX HAT

Finished Size Circumference: 8in/20cm

Hat

Using A, wind the yarn around two fingers to make a loop (Magic Ring). Ch 1, 6 sc in loop, tighten loop, sl st in first ch 1 to join—6 sts.

Rnd 1: Ch 1, (2 sc in next sc) 6 times, sl st in first ch 1 to join—12 sts.

Rnd 2: Ch 1, (sc in next sc, 2 sc in next sc) 6 times, sl st into first ch 1 to join—18 sts.

Rnd 3: Ch 1, (sc in each of next 2 sc, 2 sc in next sc) 6 times, sl st into first ch 1 to join—24 sts.

Rnd 4: Ch 1, sc in each sc, sl st into first ch 1 to join—24 sts.

Rnd 5: Ch 1, (sc in each of next 2 sc, 2 sc in next sc) 8 times, sl st into first ch 1 to join—32 sts.

Rnd 6: Ch 1, working in back loops of stitches, sc in each sc, sl st into first ch 1 to join—32 sts.

Rnds 7–9: Ch 1, sc in each sc, sl st into first ch 1 to join—32 sts.

Rnd 10: Ch 1, working in back loops of stitches, sc in each sc, sl st into first ch 1 to join—32 sts.

Fasten off. Weave in all ends.

Flower

Using white yarn, wind yarn around two fingers to make a loop (Magic Ring). Into this loop, ch 1, work (sc, dc, ch 2, dc) 5 times, sl st into first ch 1 to close ring—5 petals. Tighten loop. Thread a tapestry needle with dark gray yarn. Make a French knot in the center of the flower. Weave in all ends and sew the flower to the hat.

Princess Eugenie

DOLL

Follow the basic directions for the Large Doll, and refer to photo of Princess Eugenie on **page 14.**

Shoes: Use black yarn.

Legs/Tights: Use MC.

Shirt/Upper Body: Use color A. Wrap the sleeves ¾ of the way down the arm. Wrap the yarn five times around the neck, then stitch or wrap the triangular accents at the yoke as in the photograph.

Skirt: Cut 64 12 in/30.5cm pieces of A. Make a lark's head knot fringe over a doubled 36in/92cm piece of A. Trim the skirt to 4½in/11.5cm and tie it around the waist firmly.

Bloomers: Use color A.

Hair: Wrap one strand of color B and C held together 60 times around a 9in/23cm board. Follow the basic directions to make the hair. Sew the hair to the doll and trim.

Face: Follow the basic directions for the Large Doll, using olive green floss to embroider the colored part of the eye and brown floss for the brows.

BONUS ACCESSORY TO CROCHET

HAT

Crown

Chain 15 with black yarn.

Row 1: Sc in 2nd ch from hook, 2 sc in next ch, (sc and hdc) in next ch, hdc in next ch, 2 hdc in next ch, (hdc and dc) in next ch, dc in next 2 ch, (dc and hdc) in next ch, 2 hdc in next ch, hdc in next ch, (hdc and sc) in next ch, 2 sc in next ch, sc in last ch, turn—22 sts.

Rows 2–3: Ch 1, sc in each sc, turn.

Fasten off, leaving a tail to sew the hat to the head.

Ribbon

Chain 20.

Row 1: Sc in 2nd ch from hook and every ch across, turn—19 sts.

Rows 2–3: Ch 1, sc in each sc, turn.

Fasten off, leaving a tail to sew the ribbon to the hat.

FINISHING

Curved edge of base is front of hat.

Fold the ribbon in half and sew it down to the base, creating an open loop as shown in the picture. Weave in the ends. Sew the hat to the head.

Prince Edward, Earl of Wessex

MATERIALS

FINISHED HEIGHT 10¾in/27cm

MATERIALS

Yarn

- Knit Picks® Wool of the Andes Superwash 1.75oz/50g, 110yds/101m (100% superwash wool)†—two skeins each: #26317 Oyster Heather (MC), #26302 Dove Heather (A), #26304 Cobblestone Heather (B)

- Knit Picks® Swish Worsted 1.75oz/50g, 110yds/101m (100% superwash merino wool)—one skein each: #23876 Black (C), #24662 White (D)

- Knit Picks® Palette 1.75oz/50g, 231yds/211m (100% Peruvian Highland wool)—one ball each: #24004 Brindle Heather (E), #24242 Suede (F), #24240 Doe (G)

- Small amount of red yarn

† Two skeins of Wool of the Andes is enough yarn for the basic large doll figure if you do not use it to fill the head. You can make a ball of scrap yarn and cover it with a light covering of the Wool of the Andes. It is a rather thin yarn.

Other Tools

- Sharp scissors, a ruler, stiff cardboard, and a large, blunt-tipped tapestry needle

- Six-strand embroidery floss in black, white, bluish green, medium brown, and rose pink

- Powder blush or paint for cheeks

DOLL

Follow the basic directions for the Large Doll using MC, and refer to photo of Prince Edward on **page 64.**

Note: The kilt is constructed, then placed on the figure halfway through the construction of the jacket, so that the additional wraps of the jacket cover the kilt at the hips.

Head/Body/Leg Bundle (Make 2): Wrap MC 90 times around a 12in/30.5cm board.

Shoes: Use B.

Legs: Use A. Wrap 1.5in/4cm from the ankle to make socks. Build up the layers to make sock cuffs. Cut a small piece of red yarn and knot it onto the side of the sock to create fringe. Repeat for the other sock. Switch to MC and wrap the rest of the legs. Wrap four layers. Wrap as for bloomers to create hips.

Arm Bundle (Make 1): Wrap MC 70 times around a 9in/23cm board. Make the hands following the basic directions for the Large Doll. Wrap the rest of the arm bundle with B.

Kilt: Cut 40 12in/30.5cm pieces of A, eight pieces of C and 16 pieces of red. Cut a 24in/61cm piece of B for a foundation yarn. Using two strands for each knot, attach the knots in the following sequence: (two A, one red, one A, one red, two A, one C) four times.The horizontal stripes are created by working rows of lark's head knots across each knotted four-strand group of fringe across the entire kilt. There are four horizontal rows (two A and two red)—two are hidden under the jacket. Set aside.

Shirt/Jacket: Using color D, wrap to cover the chest for the shirt. Anchor and snip. Switch to B and wrap around the upper arms, building up layers of wraps, following the basic directions sequence to create a jacket. Build layers of wraps around the shoulders and upper arms, and then wrap two layers down the arms to build the sleeves. Trim the fringe at the bottom of the kilt. Tie it firmly onto the doll at the waist. Knot or stitch the back of the kilt closed, being careful to secure all loose yarn ends. Wrap the jacket yarn around the hips to secure the kilt, then build up the layers of the jacket at the hips and waist. Add layers of wraps from the shoulder to the hips. End with a few wraps at the waist to cinch in the center. Wrap a piece of white yarn around the neck 12 times to create the collar. Cut three 12in/30.5cm pieces of C and wrap around the white collar once, then tie in an overhand knot at the front to create a necktie. Trim and tuck the ends under the jacket to secure. Knot or embroider on three black yarn buttons at the front of the jacket.

Hair: Cut 72 9in/23cm pieces each of E, F, and G. Using one strand of each color held together as one, make a series of 36 lark's head knots around the hairline. Fill in the crown of the head with 36 knots. Trim the hair.

Face: Follow the basic directions for the Large Doll, using bluish green floss to embroider the colored part of the eye and medium brown floss for the brows.

Sophie, Countess of Wessex

FINISHED HEIGHT 10½in/26.5cm
MATERIALS

Yarn

- Knit Picks® Wool of the Andes Superwash 1.75oz/50g, 110yds/101m (100% superwash wool)—two skeins: #26317 Oyster Heather (MC)

- Knit Picks® Galileo 1.75oz/50g, 131yds/120m (50% merino wool, 50% bamboo)—one skein: #26098 Valentine (A)

- Knit Picks® Hawthorne Sport 3.5oz/100g, 258yds/236m (100% superwash wool)—one skein: #26710 Rose City (B)

- Knit Picks® Palette 1.75oz/50g, 231yds/211m (100% Peruvian Highland wool)—one skein each: #24250 Semolina (C), #24242 Suede (D), and #24252 Cornmeal (E)

Other Tools

- Sharp scissors, a ruler, stiff cardboard, and a large, blunt-tipped tapestry needle

- Six-strand embroidery floss in black, white, blue, light golden brown, and rose pink

- Silver metallic embroidery floss

- Powder blush or paint for cheeks

DOLL

Follow the basic directions for the Large Doll, wrapping MC 30 times around a 12in/30.5cm board. Refer to photo of Sophie on **page 9**.

Shoes: Use A.

Arm Bundle (Make 1): Make 60 wraps using MC. Wrap the arms with MC. After the arm bundle is inserted into the body, wrap the upper arms lightly with MC to create shoulders.

Shirt/Upper Body: Wrap one layer of MC to create a smooth upper body. Switch to A and wrap, creating the gown bodice. Wrap in sequence as in the basic directions for the Large Doll.

Bloomers: Use A.

Skirt: Cut 108 16in/41cm pieces of B. Make a lark's head knot fringe of 36 knots of three strands each knotted over a doubled 24in/61cm piece of B. Trim and tie the skirt onto the lower waist. Wrap silver floss around the waist to create a sash. Anchor and snip. If necessary, stitch or knot the skirt to the body to secure.

Hair: Using one strand of C, D, and E held together, wrap the yarn 56 times around a 9in/23cm board. Create a wig as in the basic directions for the Large Doll, making 14 bunches of 12 strands each. Attach the wig to the head. Cut six to eight 9in/23cm pieces using all three yarns held together. Make lark's head knots of three strands each in front of the wig for long layers. Coil the top hair into a chignon, and secure with a few stitches.

Face: Follow the basic directions for the Large Doll, using blue floss to embroider the colored part of the eye and light golden brown floss for the brows.

Lady Louise Windsor

FINISHED HEIGHT 9½in/24cm

MATERIALS

Yarn

- Cascade Yarns®220 Superwash® 3.5oz/100g, 220yds/200m (100% super-wash wool)—one skein each: #228 Frosted Almond (MC), #815 Black (A), #856 Aporto (B), #813 Blue Velvet (C), #820 Lemon (D), #821 Daffodil (E)

- 3yds/2.75m metallic gold yarn

Other Tools

- Sharp scissors, a ruler, stiff cardboard, and a large, blunt-tipped tapestry needle

- Six-strand embroidery floss in black, white, light golden brown, blue, and rose pink

- Powder blush or paint for cheeks

DOLL

Follow the basic directions for the Large Doll, and refer to photo of Lady Louise on **page 15**.

Head/Body/Leg Bundle (Make 2): Use MC and an 11in/28cm board.

Arm Bundle (Make 1): Use MC and an 8in/20cm board.

Shoes: Use A.

Legs: Using MC, wrap for 4in/10cm.

Shirt/Upper Body: Use B.

Skirt: Cut 60 10in/25.5cm pieces of B. Make a lark's head knot fringe over a doubled 30in/76cm piece of B. Trim the fringe to 3in/7.5cm and tie it firmly around the waist.

Shrug: Using C, wrap 15 wraps around each upper arm to create the shoulders, then wrap the yarn in a figure-8 pattern *around the right arm, across the back, around the left arm, and across the back, repeating from the * until the shape is pleasing. Anchor and snip.

Sash: Cut three 36in/91cm pieces of gold yarn. Knot them together and twist until the yarn doubles back on itself. Knot both ends to maintain the twist.

Trim ends.

Hair: Use one strand of D and one strand of E held together. Make a basic wig following the directions for the Large Doll, wrapping the two strands 60 times around a 9in/23cm board. Curl the hair by twisting clumps of the hair and steaming with an iron set to a setting appropriate for the yarn. Attach the wig to the head.

Face: Follow the basic directions for the Large Doll, using blue floss to embroider the colored part of the eye and light golden brown for the brows.

James, Viscount Severn

FINISHED HEIGHT 7½in/19cm

MATERIALS

Yarn

- Debbie Bliss® Cashmerino Aran
  1.75oz/50g, 98yds/90m (55% wool/33%
  acrylic/12% cashmere)—one skein each:
  #79 Nude (MC), #66 Mustard (A),
  #04 Navy (B)

- Debbie Bliss® Baby Cashmerino
  1.75oz/50g, 137yds/125m (55% wool/33%
  acrylic/12% cashmere)—one skein: #202
  Light Blue (C)

- Small amounts of black, medium blue, and
  white yarn

Other Tools

- Sharp scissors, a ruler, stiff cardboard, and
  a large, blunt-tipped tapestry needle

- Six-strand embroidery floss in black, white,
  blue, light brown, silver, and rose pink

- Powder blush or paint for cheeks

DOLL

Follow the basic directions for the Large Doll, and refer to photo of James on **page 15.**

Head/Body/Leg Bundle (Make 2): Wrap MC 50 times around a 6¾in/17.5cm board. Wrap a yarn ball that is 7in/18cm in circumference to stuff the head.

Shoes: Use black yarn and wrap for ¾in/2cm on each side of the constrictor knot. Fold at the ankle and follow the directions for the Large Doll to finish the shoe.

Trousers: Using B, wrap the legs for 2½in/6cm, then build up the wraps at the ankles to form the bottom of the trousers. Wrap the yarn in a figure-8 pattern as in the basic directions to form the hips until the waist and bottom are covered. Wrap the yarn around the hips and waist until the effect is pleasing. Anchor and snip. Wrap black yarn around the waist for the belt; anchor with a couple of stitches of silver floss for a buckle.

Arm Bundle (Make 1): Wrap MC 35 times around a 7in/18cm board. Use five strands for the thumb. Knot a piece of MC at each wrist to make the hand. Cover the arms with wraps of C to create the sleeves.

Shirt: Using C, wrap in sequence as for the Large Doll, covering the chest (eight wraps from the crotch to the shoulder, on both left and right shoulders, eight wraps around the midsection, eight wraps from the right shoulder to the left hip, and eight wraps from the left shoulder to the right hip). Repeat the wraps as needed for coverage. Wrap the yarn a number of times around the neck for the collar. Cut 12in/30.5cm pieces of yarn—two light blue and one medium blue—and wrap them around the white collar once, then tie in an overhand knot at the front to create a necktie. Using C, knot on buttons on the front of the shirt. Anchor and snip.

Hair: Make the wig following the basic directions for the Large Doll, wrapping A 100 times around a 5in/12.5cm board. Secure the yarn with lark's head knots in ten bundles of ten strands each. Attach the wig to the head. Cut 28 7in/18cm pieces of A. Make a series of lark's head knots (two strands of yarn knotted over two strands of the face yarn) around the hairline. Trim the hair. Stitch or wrap some of the front pieces back on each side of the forehead to hold them in place.

Face: Follow the basic directions, using blue floss to embroider the colored part of the eye and light brown floss for the brows.

CATHERINE, Duchess of Cambridge, and
PRINCE WILLIAM, Duke of Cambridge

Prince William, Duke of Cambridge

FINISHED HEIGHT 10¾in/27cm

MATERIALS

Yarn

- Cascade Yarns® 220 Superwash® 3.5oz/100g, 220yds/200m (100% superwash wool)—1 skein each: #228 Frosted Almond (MC), #815 Black (A), #809 Really Red (B), #877 Golden (C), #821 Daffodil (D)

- Small amounts of red, blue, brown, and white yarn

Other Tools

- Sharp scissors, a ruler, stiff cardboard, and a large, blunt-tipped tapestry needle

- Six-strand embroidery floss in metallic gold, black, white, blue, brown, yellow, and rose pink

- Powder blush or paint for cheeks

DOLL

Follow the basic directions for the Large Doll.

Head/Body/Leg Bundle (Make 2): Wrap MC 90 times around a 12in/30.5cm board.

Shoes: Use A.

Legs/Trousers: Using A, wrap four layers, building up layers at the bottom to form pant cuffs. Wrap as for bloomers to make the hips.

Arm Bundle (Make 1): Use MC and 70 wraps. Make the hands following the basic directions for the Large Doll. Wrap the rest of the arm bundle in B for the jacket sleeves.

Shirt/Upper Body: Using B, build up layers of wraps, following the basic directions sequence to create a jacket. Build layers of wraps around the shoulders and upper arms, and then wrap two layers down the arms to build the sleeves. Wrap around the hips to create a longer jacket. Wrap a piece of D around the neck for the collar. Use white yarn to trim the collar by wrapping a few wraps at the top and at the bottom of the yellow collar. Wrap D yarn and white yarn in a stripe sequence at each sleeve cuff as in the photograph.

Trim the sleeve cuff with a wrap of black floss at the bottom and top of the yellow cuff. Wrap brown yarn around the hips for a belt. Wrap blue yarn from shoulder to hip a number of times to create a sash. Thread a piece of black yarn into a tapestry needle. Wrapping around the existing red wraps, wrap or stitch the black yarn a few times at the top of each shoulder from neck to top of arm to create epaulets. Work one of the epaulets over the top of the blue sash.

Trim: Cut 8in/20cm pieces of embroidery floss: four blue and two white. Using a separate piece of floss as the foundation, make a lark's head knot fringe with two pieces of colored floss in this sequence: blue, white, blue. Sew the fringe to the uniform, and trim evenly so that the fringe resembles the ribbons that hold medals. A little water will tame the floss and make it easier to cut in a straight line. Make a small tassel of brown and yellow floss by making a bundle of five wraps of each color wound around three fingers. Tie a knot at the top and one around the middle of the bundle, and clip the bottom open. Trim the tassel and secure to the belt with a loop of brown floss. Using metallic floss, stitch or knot on the medals and buttons. Anchor and snip all yarn ends.

Hair: Cut 72 9in/23cm pieces each of C and D. Using one strand of each color held together, make a series of 36 lark's head knots around the hairline. Fill in the crown of the head with 36 knots. Trim the hair.

Face: Follow the basic directions for the Large Doll, using blue floss to embroider the colored part of the eye.

Catherine, Duchess of Cambridge
(Princess Kate)

FINISHED HEIGHT 10¾in/27cm

MATERIALS

- Rowan Baby Merino Silk DK 1.75oz/50g, 148yds/135m (66% wool/34% silk)—two skeins: #690 Pebble (MC)

- Rowan Pure Wool Superwash DK 3.5oz/100g, 137yds/125m (100% superwash wool)—one skein each: #101 Chalk (A)†, #110 Dust (B)

- Anchor Artiste Metallic .88oz/25gr, 100yds/109m (80% viscose, 20% metalized polyester)—one skein: #302 Pale Gold (C)

- Rowan Pure Wool Superwash Worsted 3.5oz/100g, 219yds/200m (100% superwash wool)—one skein: #102 Soft Cream (D)

- Rowan Kidsilk Haze Shine .22oz/6.25g, 11yds/10m (61% kid mohair, 27% silk, 12% cotton with crystals from Swarovski)—one ball: #634 Cream (E)

- Small amount of white yarn [to crochet tiara and veil only]

† Rowan Pure Wool Superwash Worsted, #102 Soft Cream (D) may be used instead of A for the bodice and bloomers if desired.

Other Tools

- Sharp scissors, a ruler, stiff cardboard, and a large, blunt-tipped tapestry needle

- Six-strand embroidery floss in black, white, brown, green, and rose pink

- For bouquet: Six-strand embroidery floss in green, light green, white, yellow, and cream

- Powder blush or paint for cheeks

- Size D (3mm) crochet hook [to crochet tiara, veil, and bouquet]

DOLL

Head/Body/Leg Bundle (Make 1): Follow the basic directions for the Large Doll wrapping MC 75 times around a 12in/30.5cm board. Use MC to wrap the legs. Refer to the photo of Princess Kate on **page 12.**

Shoes: Use C.

Arm Bundle (Make 1): Wrap MC 55 times around a 9in/23cm board. Wrap the arms with MC. After the arm bundle is inserted into the body, wrap the upper arms lightly to create shoulders. Wrap the arms from shoulder to wrist with C to create sleeves.

Bloomers: Use MC.

Shirt/Upper Body: Wrap one layer of MC to create a smooth upper body. Switch to A, and wrap, creating the gown bodice. Wrap in sequence as in the basic directions for the Large Doll. Switch to C. Wrap from the right shoulder to the crotch 15 times, then from the left shoulder to the crotch 15 times. Wrap around the waist several times to create the waistband.

Skirts (Make 2): Cut 120 16in/41cm pieces of D. Make a lark's head fringe knot skirt of 20 knots of three strands each knotted over a doubled 24in/61cm piece of yarn. Trim and tie it onto the lower waist. Make a second skirt and tie on at the waist just above the first skirt. This creates fullness. If desired, stitch or knot the skirt to the body to secure.

Hair: Using one strand of B, wrap the yarn 120 times around a 9in/23cm board. Make a wig as in the basic directions for the Large Doll, making 12 bunches of ten strands each. Trim the hair.

Face: Follow the basic directions for the Large Doll, using green floss to embroider the colored part of the eye and brown floss for brows. If desired, embroider an extra line of split stitches (made from two strands of black thread) just above the green part of the eye to give the effect of eyeliner.

TIARA AND VEIL

Finished Size: 9½in/24cm in circumference

Stitch Glossary

MB: Make bobble. Yo, insert hook from front to back of next st as if to make a dc, pull through one loop, (yo, insert hook in same st from front to back, pull through loop) three times, yo and pull through all nine loops on hook. Bobble made.

Tiara

Using C, ch 65.

Row 1: Sc in second ch from hook and in each sc across, turn—64 sts.

Row 2: *Ch 1, sc in next 2 sc [sc in next sc, sl st in next sc, MB in next sc, ch 1, skip next 2 sc, trc in next sc, then, in space created between bobble and trc, work (sl st, ch 1, 2 sc), hdc back in same st as trc] 4 times, sc in next sc, sl st in next sc, MB in next sc, ch 1, skip next 2 sc, trc in next sc, then, in space created between bobble and trc, work (ch1, 2 hdc, 2 sc), hdc back in same st as trc. Fasten off.* Turn work. Attach yarn at other end of Row 1 and repeat from * to *.

Row 3: With right side facing, attach yarn to 2nd hdc of large center right hand swirl. Ch 1, sl st into corresponding hdc of other large swirl. Ch 1, turn, MB in ch st between the two swirls. Fasten off.

FINISHING

Stitch two back ends together. Weave in ends.

Veil

With white, ch 16 for a foundation chain. Fasten off.

Cut 16 24in/61cm pieces of E. Tie one piece into each foundation ch st with a knot at the top of each piece. Stitch the veil to the underside front edge of the tiara. Trim if desired.

FLORAL BOUQUET

Refer to the photo of Princess Kate on page 68.

Bouquet Holder

Rnd 1: Using green floss, wind yarn around two fingers to make a loop (Magic Ring).

Ch 1, 6 sc in loop, tighten loop, sl st into first ch 1 to join—6 sts.

Rnd 2: Ch 1, 2 sc in each sc, sl st in first ch 1 to join—12 sts.

Rnd 3: Ch 1, 2 hdc in each sc, sl st 1 in first ch 1 to join—24 sts.

Rnd 4: Ch 1, 2 hdc in each sc, sl st 1 in first ch 1 to join—48 sts.

Rnd 5: Ch 1, [3 sc in next sc, (hdc, dc, and hdc in next sc), sl st in next sc] 16 times, sl st 1 into ch 1 to join. Fasten off.

Small Flowers

Using cream floss, wind the yarn around two fingers to make a loop (Magic Ring). Ch 1, (sc, ch 1, sc) 5 times in loop, tighten loop, sl st into first ch 1 to close ring. Cut the floss tail to 3in/7.5cm to be used later for the bouquet handle.

Large Flowers

Using yellow floss, wind the yarn around two fingers to make a loop (Magic Ring). Ch 1, 7 sc in loop, tighten loop, sl st into first sc to join—7 sts.

Next Rnd Switch to white or cream floss, ch 1, (work sc, ch 2, and sc in next sc) 7 times, sl st into ch 1 to join. Fasten off. Cut the floss tail to 3in/7.5cm to be used later for the bouquet handle.

Knot Flowers (Make a few in light green and yellow)

Leaving a 3in/7.5cm tail at beg of work, ch 2, then MB in second ch from hook. Pull gently to tighten knot. Ch 1, then end off, leaving 3in/7.5 tail.

Assembling Bouquet

Grasp all of the flowers together by their 3in/7.5cm tails. Pinch this bundle of stems together and pull it through the hole in the center of the bouquet holder. Anchor a piece of green floss, and wrap the stems firmly for 1in/2.5 cm. Anchor and snip the green floss end. Use a piece of floss and stitch to anchor the bouquet to the hand.

Prince George

FINISHED HEIGHT 6in/15cm

MATERIALS

Yarn

- Debbie Bliss® Cashmerino Aran 1.75oz/50g, 98yds/90m (55% wool/33% acrylic/12% cashmere)—one skein each: #79 Nude (MC), #64 Cowslip (A)

- Debbie Bliss® Baby Cashmerino 1.75oz/50g, 137yds/125m (55% wool/33% acrylic/12% cashmere)—one skein each: #27 Denim (B), #34 Red (C)

- Small amounts of black and white yarn

Other Tools

- Sharp scissors, a ruler, stiff cardboard, and a large, blunt-tipped tapestry needle

- Six-strand embroidery floss in black, white, light golden brown, and rose pink

- Powder blush or paint for cheeks

DOLL

Follow the basic directions for the Large Doll.

Head/Body/Leg Bundle (Make 2): Wrap MC 45 times around a 7in/18cm board. Wrap a yarn ball that is 6½in/16.5cm in circumference to stuff the head.

Shoes: Use black yarn and wrap for ½in/1cm on each side of the constrictor knot. Fold at the ankle and follow the directions for the Large Doll to finish the shoe.

Legs/Socks: Using MC, wrap the legs for 1½in/4cm. Switch to B and wrap for ¼in/.6cm around each ankle to create socks. Anchor and snip.

Arm Bundle (Make 1): Wrap MC 30 times around a 5in/13cm board. Use four strands for the thumb. Cover the arms with two layers of wraps of B for the sleeves.

Pullover Sweater: Using B, wrap in sequence as for the Large Doll, covering the chest (eight wraps from the crotch to the shoulder, on both left and right shoulders, eight wraps around the midsection, eight wraps from the right shoulder to the left hip,

and eight wraps from the left shoulder to the right hip). Repeat the wraps as needed for coverage. Wrap white yarn a number of times around the neck for the collar. Anchor and snip.

Shorts: Create the hips by wrapping C in a figure-8 pattern around both legs until the waist and bottom are covered. Wrap each leg down from the waist for 1in/2.5cm to create shorts. Wrap the yarn around the hips and waist until the effect is pleasing. Anchor and snip.

Hair: Wrap A 90 times around a 5in/12.5cm board. Make the wig following the basic directions for the Large Doll, making ten knots of nine strands each. Attach the wig to the head. Cut 28 7in/18cm pieces of A. Using two pieces of yarn knotted over two strands of the face yarn, make a series of lark's head knots around the hairline. Trim the hair.

Face: Follow the basic directions, using blue floss to embroider the colored part of the eye and light golden brown floss for the brows.

Princess Charlotte

FINISHED HEIGHT 4½in/11.5cm

MATERIALS

Yarn

- Cascade Yarns® 220 Superwash® 3.5oz/100g, 220yds/200m (100% superwash merino wool)—one skein each: #228 Frosted Almond (MC), #853 Butterscotch (A)

- Cascade Yarns® 220 Superwash® Sport 1.75oz/50g, 136yds/125m (100% superwash merino wool)—one skein each: #894 Strawberry Cream (B), #836 Pink Ice (C)

- Small amounts of dark gray and white yarn

Other Tools

- Sharp scissors, a ruler, stiff cardboard, and a large, blunt-tipped tapestry needle

- Six-strand embroidery floss in black, white, soft brown, blue, and peachy pink

- Powder blush or paint for cheeks

DOLL

Follow the basic directions for the Large Doll.

Head/Body/Leg Bundle (Make 2): Wrap MC 35 times around a 5in/13cm board. Wrap a yarn ball that is 5in/13cm in circumference to stuff the head.

Shoes: Use dark gray yarn and wrap for ½in/.5cm on each side of the constrictor knot. Fold at the ankle and follow the directions for the Large Doll to finish the shoe.

Legs/Socks: Using MC, wrap the legs for 1in/2.5cm. Switch to white yarn and wrap two times around each ankle. Anchor and snip.

Arm Bundle (Make 1): Wrap MC 20 times around a 3½in/9cm board. Use three strands for the thumb. Cover the arms with MC.

Shirt: Using B, wrap in sequence as for the Large Doll, covering the chest (eight wraps from the crotch to the shoulder, on both left and right shoulders, eight wraps around the midsection, eight wraps from the right shoulder to the left hip, and eight wraps from the left shoulder to the right hip). Repeat the wraps as needed for coverage. Anchor and snip.

Bloomers: Wrap B eight times around the top of each leg, then wrap the yarn in a figure-8 pattern around both legs until the waist and bottom are covered. Wrap the yarn around the hips and waist until the effect is pleasing. Anchor and snip.

Skirt: Cut 40 5in/12.5cm pieces of C. Create a lark's head knot fringe of 20 knots of two strands each knotted over a doubled 24in/61cm piece of C. Tie it around the waist and trim the yarn. Use the tapestry needle to separate the yarn plies.

Hair: Following the basic directions for the Large Doll, wrap A 50 times around a 5in/12.5cm board. Following the directions for the Large Doll, create a wig by making ten knots of six strands each. Attach the wig to the head. Using a piece of C, stitch or wrap some of the front pieces of hair on one side of the forehead to hold them in place.

Face: The eyes are French knots of doubled six-strand pieces of black floss, surrounded by a lazy daisy stitch of a six-strand piece of blue floss. The white eye accent is two strands of white floss doubled to make a small straight stitch. The mouth is made from two straight stitches of two strands doubled of light peachy pink floss. The brows are soft brown.

Prince Henry of Wales
(Prince Harry)

FINISHED HEIGHT 11in/28cm

MATERIALS

Yarn

- Lion Brand® Vanna's Choice® 3.5oz/100g, 170yds/156m (100% acrylic)—one skein each: #860-123 Beige (MC), #860-153 Black (A), #860-124 Toffee (B), #860-135 Rust (C), #860-130 Honey (D)

- Lion Brand® Glitterspun® 16ft/5m (80% polyester, 20% nylon)—one card #605-170 Gold (E)

- Lion Brand® Vanna's Choice® Baby 3.5oz/100g, 170yds/156m (100%acrylic)— one skein: # 840-108 Bluebell (F) [to crochet beret only]

- Small amounts of white, black, red, blue, soft reddish-brown, and light gray yarn

Other Tools

- Sharp scissors, a ruler, stiff cardboard, and a large, blunt-tipped tapestry needle

- Six-strand embroidery floss in black, white, blue, rose pink, and metallic gold

- For ribbons: Six-strand embroidery floss in red, white, blue, and medium blue

- Powder blush or paint for cheeks

- Size H-8 (5mm) crochet hook [to crochet beret]

DOLL

Follow the basic directions for the Large Doll.

Head/Body/Leg Bundle (Make 2): Wrap MC 65 times around a 12in/30.5cm board.

Shoes: Use A.

Legs/Trousers/Hips: Use B. Wrap four layers, building up layers at bottom to form pant cuffs. Wrap as for bloomers to create the hips.

Arm Bundle (Make 2): Wrap MC 45 times around a 9in/23cm board. Wrap ½in/1cm at the wrists in C. Wrap the rest of the arm bundle in B for the jacket sleeves.

Shirt/Vest/Jacket: Using white yarn, wrap to cover the chest for the shirt, anchor and snip. Switch to B, and wrap around the upper arms, building up layers of wraps, following the basic directions sequence to create a jacket. Build layers of wraps around the shoulders and upper arms, and then wrap two layers down the arms to build the sleeves. Wrap around the hips to create a longer jacket. End with a few wraps at the waist to cinch in the center. Wrap A 12 times around the waist for a belt, then wrap three times from shoulder to waist. Anchor and snip. Thread a tapestry needle with one strand of B and one strand of E. Anchor in an inconspicuous place and bring up at the neck and shoulder. Wrap one or two times at the shoulder to create a base, then wrap around the stitch just made to make an epaulet. Anchor and snip; repeat for the other shoulder. Wrap a piece of white yarn around the neck 12 times to create a collar. Cut three 12 in/30.5cm pieces of light gray yarn and wrap around the white collar once, then tie in an overhand knot at the front to create a necktie. Trim and tuck ends under the vest to secure.

Trim: Cut ten 8in/20cm pieces of ribbon-color embroidery floss. Using one piece of floss as the foundation, make a lark's head knot fringe with nine pieces of colored floss. Sew the fringe to the uniform, and trim evenly so the fringe resembles the ribbons that hold medals. A little water will "tame" the floss and make it easier to cut in a straight line. Using E, make buttons with tied or embroidered knots, and wrap two times around the belt to create a buckle. Anchor and snip.

Hair: The Prince's hair is made in two parts. The hair is rooted to the head at the hairline with lark's head knots, then a fringe is sewn to the crown of the head for additional coverage. Wrap one strand each of C and D held together, 40 times around a 5in/12.5cm board. Cut across the board evenly, creating 80 strands of yarn, each 10in/25cm long. Attach the hair with lark's head knots. There are 40 knots, each using two strands of yarn (one of each color), forming a circle around the doll's head. Position the knots so they create the appearance of a natural hairline. The Prince has 30 knots around his head, and a double row of knots along the front. Then, following the basic directions for the Large Doll, make a wig by wrapping one strand each of color C and D held together 50 times around a 5in/12.5cm board. Knot across the fringe, making ten bunches of ten strands. Cut the fringe open and fold in half. Sew the center part, and stitch it down to the crown of the head. Trim all hair.

Face: Follow the basic directions for the Large Doll, using blue floss to embroider the colored part of the eye and soft, reddish-brown floss for the brows.

BERET

Finished Diameter (flattened): 5in/13cm

Rnd 1: Using F, wind the yarn around two fingers to make a loop (Magic Ring). Ch 1, 6 sc in loop, tighten loop, sl st in ch1 to join—6 sts.

Rnd 2: Ch 1, (sc in next sc, 2 sc in next sc) 3 times, sl st in first ch 1 to join—9 sts.

Rnd 3: Ch 1, (2 sc in next sc) 9 times, sl st in first ch 1 to join—18 sts.

Rnd 4: Ch 1, (sc in next 2 sc, 2 sc in next sc) 6 times, sl st in first ch 1 to join—24 sts.

Rnd 5: Ch 1, (sc in next 3 sc, 2 sc in next sc) 6 times, sl st in first ch 1 to join—30 sts.

Rnd 6: Ch 1, (sc in next 4 sc, 2 sc in next sc) 6 times, sl st in first ch 1 to join—36 sts.

Rnd 7: Ch 1, (sc in next 5 sc, 2 sc in next sc) 6 times, sl st in first ch 1 to join—42 sts.

Rnd 8: Ch 1, sc in next sc, (sc in next 4 sc, 2 sc in next sc) 8 times, sc in next sc, sl st in first ch 1 to join—50 sts.

Rnd 9: Ch 1, (sc next 4 sc, 2 sc in next sc) 10 times, sl st in first ch 1 to join—60 sts.

Rnd 10: Ch 1, sc in each sc, sl st in first ch 1 to join—60 sts.

Rnd 11: Ch 1, (sc in next 4 sc, sc2tog) 10 times, sl st in first ch 1 to join—50 sts.

Rnd 12: Ch 1, (sc in next 3 sc, sc2tog) 10 times, sl st in first ch 1 to join—40 sts.

Rnd 13: Ch 1, (sc in next 6 sc, sc2tog) 5 times, sl st in first ch 1 to join—35 sts.

Rnd 14: Ch 1, (sc in next 5 sc, sc2tog) 5 times, sl st in first ch 1 to join—30 sts.

Rnds 15 and 16: Ch 1, sc in each sc, sl st in first ch 1 to join—30 sts.

Switch to black yarn.

Rnd 17: Ch 1, sc in each sc, sl st in first ch 1 to join—30 sts.

Patch

Using blue yarn, ch 4.

Row 1: Sc in second chain from hook and next 2 ch, turn—3 sts.

Row 2: Ch 1, sc in each sc, turn.

Row 3: Switch to red yarn. Ch 1, sc in each sc, turn.

Row 4: Switch to blue yarn. Ch 1, sc in each sc, turn. End off.

FINISHING

Block lightly, weave in the ends. Thread a tapestry needle with embroidery floss and make a straight stitch star on patch. Sew patch to side of beret.

Peter Phillips

FINISHED HEIGHT 10¾in/27cm

MATERIALS

Yarn

- Bernat® Super Value 7oz/197g, 426yds/389m (100% acrylic)—one ball each: #53010 Oatmeal (MC), #07421 Black (A), #53042 Dark Gray (B), #8879 Sky (C), #7483 Walnut (D)

- Lion Brand® Vanna's Choice® 3.5oz/100g, 170yds/156m (100% acrylic)—one skein: #860-404 Dark Gray Heather (E)

Other Tools

- Sharp scissors, a ruler, stiff cardboard, and a large, blunt-tipped tapestry needle

- Six-strand embroidery floss in black, white, blue, green, and rose pink

- Powder blush or paint for cheeks

- Size H-8 (5mm) crochet hook [to crochet top hat]

DOLL

Follow the basic directions for the Large Doll.

Head/Body/Leg Bundle (Make 2): Wrap MC 65 times around a 12in/30.5cm board.

Shoes: Use A.

Legs/Trousers: Use B. Wrap four layers, building up layers at the bottom to form pant cuffs. Wrap as for bloomers to make the hips.

Arm Bundle (Make 1): Wrap MC 45 times around a 9in/23cm board. Wrap ½in/1cm at the wrists in C. Wrap the rest of the arm bundle in B for the jacket sleeves.

Shirt/Vest/Jacket: Wrap C to cover the chest for the shirt; anchor and snip. Switch to gold yarn, and wrap from the right shoulder to the crotch, and over the left shoulder a few times to create the vest. Anchor and snip, then switch to A, and wrap around the upper arms, building up layers of wraps, following the basic direction sequence to create a jacket. Build layers of wraps around the shoulders and upper arms, and then wrap two layers down

the arms to build sleeves. Wrap around the hips to create a tuxedo. End with a few wraps at the waist to cinch in the center. Wrap a piece of white yarn around the neck 12 times to create a collar. Cut three 12in/30.5cm pieces of light yellow yarn and wrap around the white collar once, then tie in an overhand knot at the front to create a necktie. Trim and tuck ends under the vest to secure. Double knot, then trim the ends of a piece of white yarn onto the jacket for a boutonniere flower, then knot a doubled piece of green embroidery floss under the white knot to make leaves. Trim to size.

Hair: Make a basic wig as in the directions for the Large Doll using D, wrapping 77 times around a 7in/18cm board. Knot 11 bunches of seven strands. Sew the wig to the doll. Cut 40 pieces 6in/15cm long, and make two-strand lark's head knots around the hairline, in front of the wig. Trim all the hair.

Face: Follow the basic directions for the Large Doll, using blue floss to embroider the colored part of the eye and brown floss for the brows.

BONUS ACCESSORY TO CROCHET

TOP HAT

Finished Height: 3in/7.5cm

Crown

Using B, wind yarn around two fingers to make a loop (Magic Ring).

Rnd 1: Ch 1, 6 sc in loop, tighten the loop, sl st in first ch 1 to join—6 sts.

Rnd 2: Ch 1, (sc in next sc, 2 sc in next sc) 3 times, sl st in first ch 1 to join—9 sts.

Rnd 3: Ch 1, (2 sc in next sc) 9 times, sl st in first ch 1 to join—18 sts.

Rnd 4: Ch 1, (sc in next 2 sc, 2 sc in next sc) 6 times, sl st in first ch 1 to join—24 sts.

Rnd 5: Ch 1, (sc in next 3 sc, 2 sc in next sc) 6 times, sl st in first ch 1 to join—30 sts.

Rnd 6: Ch 1, (sc in next 4 sc, 2 sc in next sc) 6 times, sl st in first ch 1 to join—36 sts.

Rnd 7: Ch 1, (sc in next 5 sc, 2 sc in next sc) 6 times, sl st in first ch 1 to join—42 sts.

Rnd 8: Ch 1, sc in back loop of each sc, sl st in first ch 1 to join—42 sts.

Rnds 9–13: Ch 1, sc in each sc, sl st in first ch 1 to to join—42 sts.

Rnd 14: Ch 1, (sc in next 5 sc, sc2tog) 6 times, sl st in first ch 1 to join—36 sts.

Rnds 15–16: Ch 1, sc in each sc, sl st in first ch 1 to join—36 sts.

Switch to black yarn.

Rnd 17: Ch 1, sc in back loop of each sc, sl st into first ch 1 to join—36 sts.

Rnds 18–19: Ch 1, sc in each sc, sl st into first ch 1 to join—36 sts.

Switch to MC.

Brim

Rnd 1: Ch 1, sc in back loop of each sc, sl st in first ch 1 to join—36 sts.

Rnd 2: Ch 1, (sc in next 3 sc, 2 sc in next sc) 9 times, sl st in first sc to join rnd—45 sts.

Rnd 3: Ch 1, (sc in next 4 sc, 2 sc in next sc) 9 times, sl st in first sc to join rnd—54 sts.

Rnd 4: Ch 1, sc in each sc, sl st in first sc to join rnd—54 sts.

Rnd 5: Ch 1, sl st in back loop of each sc, sl st into first sl st to join rnd—54 sts.

Fasten off.

FINISHING

Block lightly, weave in the ends. Roll the sides of the brim up.

FINISHED HEIGHT 6½in/16.5cm

MATERIALS

Yarn

- Knit Picks® Wool of the Andes Superwash 1.75oz/50g, 110yds/101m (100% superwash wool)—one skein each: #26317 Oyster Heather (MC)

- Knit Picks® Swish DK Yarn 1.75oz/50g, 123yds/112m (100% superwash merino wool)—one skein each: #24962 Carnation (A), #26060 Rouge (B)

- Knit Picks® Palette 1.75oz/50g, 231yds/21m (100% Peruvian Highland wool)—one skein each: #24250 Semolina (C), #24252 Cornmeal (D)

- Small amounts of white and black yarn

Other Tools

- Sharp scissors, a ruler, stiff cardboard, and a large, blunt-tipped tapestry needle

- Small amounts of white and black yarn

- Six-strand embroidery floss in black, white, light golden brown, dark gray, and rose pink

- Powder blush or paint for cheeks

DOLL

Follow the basic directions for the Large Doll.

Head/Body/Leg Bundle (Make 2): Wrap MC 45 times around a 7in/18cm board. Wrap a yarn ball that is 6in/15cm in circumference to stuff the head.

Shoes: Use black yarn and wrap for ½in/1cm on each side of the constrictor knot. Fold at the ankle and follow the directions for the Large Doll to finish the shoe.

Legs/Socks: Wrap the legs for 2in/1.5cm using MC. Switch to white yarn and wrap for ¼in/.5cm around each ankle. Anchor and snip.

Bloomers: Use white yarn.

Arm Bundle (Make 1): Wrap MC 30 times around a 5in/12.5cm board. Use four strands for the thumb. Cover the arms with wraps of A.

Shirt/Cardigan: Using white yarn, wrap in sequence as for the Large Doll, covering the chest (eight wraps from the crotch to the shoulder, on both the left and right shoulders, eight wraps around the midsection, eight wraps from the right shoulder to the left hip, eight wraps from the left shoulder to the right hip). Wrap a number of times around the neck for the collar. Anchor and snip. Switch to color A and wrap in the same way, repeating the sequence as needed for coverage. Do not cover all of the white layer at the yoke. Anchor and snip. Thread a tapestry needle with B and make two French knot buttons on the center of the cardigan.

Skirt: Cut 40 6in/15cm pieces of B and make a lark's head knot fringe, using two pieces of yarn for each of the 20 knots, knotted over a doubled 24in/61cm piece of yarn. Tie the skirt firmly around the waist and trim evenly at the bottom edge.

Continue with these directions for Isla's Hair and Face:

Hair: Holding one strand each of C and D together as one, wrap 50 times around a 5in/12.5cm board. Following the basic directions for the Large Doll, create a wig by making ten knots of six strands each. Attach the wig to the head. Using a piece of B, stitch or wrap some of the front pieces of hair on one side of the forehead to hold them in place.

Face: Follow the basic directions for the Large Doll, using dark gray floss to embroider the colored part of the eye and light golden brown floss for the brows.

Savannah Phillips

FINISHED HEIGHT 6½in/16cm

MATERIALS

Yarn

- Knit Picks® Wool of the Andes Superwash 1.75oz/50g, 110yds/101m (100% superwash wool)—one skein each: #26317 Oyster Heather (MC)

- Knit Picks® Swish DK Yarn 1.75oz/50g, 123yds/112m (100% superwash merino wool)—one skein each: #26062 Wonderland Heather (A), #25585 Rainforest Heather (B)

- Knit Picks Palette® 1.75oz/50g, 231yds/21m (100% Peruvian Highland wool)—one skein each: #24250 Semolina (C), and #24252 Cornmeal (D)

- Small amounts of white and black yarn

Other Tools

- Sharp scissors, a ruler, stiff cardboard, and a large, blunt-tipped tapestry needle

- Small amounts of white and black yarn

- Six-strand embroidery floss in black, white, light golden brown, dark blue, and rose pink

- Powder blush or paint for cheeks

DOLL

Follow the basic directions for the Large Doll, using the same instructions as for Isla Phillips, except for the Hair and Face.

Continue with these directions for Savannah's Hair and Face:

Hair: Holding one strand each of C and D together as one, wrap 50 times around a 5in/12.5cm board. Following the basic directions for the Large Doll, create a wig by making ten knots of six strands each. Attach the wig to the head. Stitch or wrap back some of the front pieces on one side of the forehead to hold them in place. The headband is made from four 12in/30.5cm strands of A wrapped around the head and knotted beneath.

Face: Follow the basic directions for the Large Doll, using dark blue floss to embroider the colored part of the eye and light golden brown floss for the brows.

FINISHED HEIGHT 10¾in /27cm

MATERIALS

Yarn

- Cascade Yarns® 220 Superwash® 3.5oz/100g, 220yds/200m (100% super-wash wool)—one skein each: #228 Frosted Almond (MC), #815 Black (A), #1946 Silver Gray (B), #813 Blue Velvet (C), #820 Lemon (D), #821 Daffodil (E)

- Small amounts of red, blue, brown, and white yarn

Other Tools

- Sharp scissors, a ruler, stiff cardboard, and a large, blunt-tipped tapestry needle

- Six-strand embroidery floss in black, gold, light golden brown, white, blue, and rose pink

- Powder blush or paint for cheeks

- Size G-6 (4mm) crochet hook [to crochet hat]

DOLL

Follow the basic directions for the Large Doll.

Head/Body/Leg Bundle (Make 2): Wrap MC 80 times around a 12in/30.5cm board.

Boots: Use A to wrap the shoe portion, then wrap the legs in B; switch back to A to wrap the boot tops up to the knee. Layer the wraps so that the boot tops are wider than the legs. Anchor and snip all yarn ends.

Legs/Stirrup Pants: Use B. Wrap as for bloomers to create the hips.

Arm Bundle (Make 1): Wrap MC 60 times around a 9in/23cm board. Wrap the rest of the arm bundle in C for the jacket sleeves.

Shirt/Upper Body: Use C, building up the wraps to create a jacket. Wrap around the hips to create a longer riding jacket. Place four strands of red yarn around the neck, tucking the ends into the neck to create a collar. Cut eight 20in/51cm pieces of white yarn and wrap around the neck once, then tie in an overhand knot at the front to create an ascot. Bring the ends to the back and knot to secure. Wrap or embroider using one strand of red yarn for red pocket tops and badge. Embroider or knot buttons using gold floss. Anchor and snip all yarn ends.

Hair: Use one strand each of D and E held together. Make a basic wig following the directions for the Large Doll, wrapping the strands 60 times around a 9in/23cm board. Attach the wig to the head. Braid the front nine strands of hair on each side. Make a low ponytail tied with a piece of yarn.

Face: Follow the basic directions for the Large Doll, using blue floss to embroider the colored part of the eye and light golden brown floss for the brows.

BONUS ACCESSORY TO CROCHET

EQUESTRIAN HAT

Finished Size: 2¾in/7cm

Crown

With A and size G-6 crochet hook, ch 46, sl st into the first ch to form a ring.

Rnds 1–7: Ch 1, sc in 45 ch, sl st in first ch 1 to join—45 sts.

Rnd 8: Ch 1, (sc in next 7 ch, sc2tog) 5 times, sl st in first ch 1 to join—40 sts.

Rnd 9: Ch 1, (sc in next 6 sc, sc2tog) 5 times, sl st in first ch 1 to join—35 sts.

Rnd 10: Ch 1, (sc in next 5 sc, sc2tog) 5 times, sl st in first ch 1 to join—30 sts.

Rnd 11: Ch 1, (sc in next 4 sc, sc2tog) 5 times, sl st in first ch 1 to join—25 sts.

Rnd 12: Ch 1, (sc in next 3 sc, sc2tog) 5 times, sl st in first ch 1 to join—20 sts.

Rnd 13: Ch 1, (sc in next 2 sc, sc2tog) 5 times, sl st in first ch 1 to join—15 sts.

Rnd 14: Ch 1, (sc in next sc, sc2tog) 5 times, sl st in first ch 1 to join—10 sts.

Rnd 15 : Ch 1, (2sctog) 5 times, sl st into first ch 1 to join—5 sts.

Rnd 16: Draw up a loop in each of the 5 sts from the previous rnd, yo and draw through all the loops on the hook—1 st remains.

Next Row—Topknot: Draw up six loops evenly spaced around the previous rnd; yo and pull yarn through all 6 loops, ch 1, then cut yarn leaving a tail. Fasten off. Draw firmly to tighten knot.

Bill

Attach the yarn to the front of the crown. Sc in 14 ch at bottom edge. Turn.

Rows 1–4: Ch 1, sc in next sc, 2sctog, sc to last 3 sts, 2sctog, sc in last sc, turn—6 sc at end of Row 4.

Row 5 (Fold Row): Ch 1, sc in back loop of each sc, turn.

Rows 6–9: Ch 1, sc in next sc, 2 sc in next sc, sc to last 2 sts, 2 sc in next sc, sc in last sc, turn—14 sc at end of Row 9. Fasten off, leaving a tail. Fold the bill at the fold line and sew the edges together to create a double thickness.

FINISHING

Block lightly, weave in the ends.

Mia Tindall

FINISHED HEIGHT 6in/15cm

MATERIALS

Yarn

- Debbie Bliss® Cashmerino Aran
  1.75oz/50g, 98yds/90m (55% wool/33%
  acrylic/12% cashmere)—one skein each:
  #79 Nude (MC), #64 Cowslip (A)

- Debbie Bliss® Baby Cashmerino
  1.75oz/50g, 137yds/125m (55% wool/33%
  acrylic/12% cashmere)—one skein each:
  #27 Denim (B), #93 Clematis (C)

- Small amounts of white and black yarn

Other Tools

- Sharp scissors, a ruler, stiff cardboard, and
  a large, blunt-tipped tapestry needle

- Six-strand embroidery floss in black, white,
  light golden brown, blue, and rose pink

- Powder blush or paint for cheeks

DOLL

Follow the basic directions for the Large Doll.

Head/Body/Leg Bundle (Make 2): Wrap MC 45
times around a 7in/18cm board. Wrap a yarn ball that
is 6½in/16.5cm in circumference to stuff the head.

Shoes: Use black yarn and wrap for ½in/1cm on
each side of the constrictor knot. Fold at the ankle
and follow the directions for the Large Doll to finish
the shoe.

Legs/Socks: Wrap the legs for 1½in/4cm using MC.
Switch to white yarn and wrap for ¼in/.6cm around
each ankle. Anchor and snip.

Arm Bundle (Make 1): Wrap MC 30 times around
a 5in/13cm board. Use four strands for the thumb.
Cover the arms with wraps of C.

Sweater: Using C, wrap in sequence as for the
Large Doll, covering the chest (eight wraps from
the crotch to the shoulder, on both the left and
right shoulders, eight wraps around the midsection,
eight wraps from the right shoulder to the left hip,
eight wraps from the left shoulder to the right hip).

Repeat the wraps as needed for coverage. Wrap
white yarn a number of times around the neck for
a collar. Anchor and snip. Thread a tapestry needle
with C. Embroider French knots or hand tie knots
for buttons on the front of the sweater if desired.

Bloomers: Using B, create hips by wrapping in a
figure-8 pattern around both legs until the waist and
bottom are covered. Wrap the yarn around the hips
and waist until the effect is pleasing. Anchor and snip.

Skirt: Cut 44 5in/12.5cm pieces of B. Create a lark's
head knot fringe of 22 knots of two strands each
knotted over a doubled 24in/61cm piece of yarn.
Tie the skirt around the waist and trim.

Hair: Wrap A 90 times around a 6in/15cm board
and make a wig following the basic directions for
the Large Doll with ten knots of nine strands each.
Attach the wig to the head. With C, stitch or wrap
back some of the front pieces on both sides of the
forehead to hold them in place.

Face: Follow the basic directions for the Large Doll,
using blue floss to embroider the colored part of
the eye and light golden brown floss for the brows.

TO MAKE
QUEEN ELIZABETH'S
HANDBAG,
SEE PAGE 48.

QUEEN ELIZABETH II
and her great-granddaughter,
MIA TINDALL

Yeoman Warder

FINISHED HEIGHT 11in/28cm

MATERIALS

Yarn

- Cascade Yarn® 220 Superwash® 3.5oz/100g, 220yds/200m (100% superwash wool)—one skein each: #228 Frosted Almond (MC), #815 Black (A), #809 Really Red (B) , #853 Butterscotch (C)

- Cascade Yarns® Pluscious 3.5oz/100g, 148.7yds/136m (100% polyester)—one skein: #19 Caviar (D) [to crochet bearskin hat only]

- Small amounts of white yarn

Other Tools

- Sharp scissors, a ruler, stiff cardboard, and a large, blunt-tipped tapestry needle

- Six-strand embroidery floss in black, white, blue, light golden brown, and rose pink

- Powder blush or paint for cheeks

- Small amounts of gold metallic floss or yarn [to crochet bearskin hat]

- Size H-8 (5mm) crochet hook [to crochet bearskin hat]

- Fiberfill to stuff top of hat (optional)

DOLL

Follow the basic directions for the Large Doll.

Head/Body/Leg Bundle (Make 2): Use MC to make two bundles of 90 wraps each.

Shoes: Use color B.

Legs/Trousers: Use color A. Wrap four layers, building up layers at the bottom to form pant cuffs. Wrap as for bloomers to create the hips.

Arm Bundle (Make 1): Use MC and 70 wraps. Make the hands, then wrap the rest of arm in B for jacket sleeves.

Shirt/Upper Body: Use B, building up layers of wraps, following the basic directions sequence to create a jacket. Build layers of wraps around the shoulders and upper arms, then wrap two layers down the arms to build the sleeves. Wrap around the hips to create a longer jacket. Wrap the sleeve cuffs and collar with A. Wrap white yarn around the waist for a belt, and embroider or knot white yarn buttons.

Hair: The Guard's hair is made in two parts. The hair is rooted to the head at the hairline with lark's head knots; then a fringe is sewn to the crown of the head for additional coverage. Wrap C 60 times around a 5in/12.5cm board. Cut across the board evenly, creating 60 10in/25cm strands of yarn. Follow the basic directions for the Large Doll to attach the hair with lark's head knots. There are 30 knots, each using two strands of yarn, forming a circle around the doll's head. Position the knots so that they create the appearance of a natural hairline. Then make a fringe, following the basic directions for the Large Doll, by wrapping C 100 times around a 5in/12.5cm board. Knot across the fringe, making ten bunches of ten strands. Cut the fringe open and fold in half. Sew the center part, and stitch the wig to the crown of the head. Trim all hair.

Face: Follow the basic directions for the Large Doll, using blue floss to embroider the colored part of the eye and light golden brown floss for the brows.

BEARSKIN HAT

Finished Height: 4½in/11cm

The hat is crocheted holding one strand of D and A together.

Ch 26, sl st in the first ch to make a ring.

Rnds 1–12: Ch 1, sc in each of 25 ch, sl st in first ch 1 to join—25 sts.

Rnd 13: Ch 1, (sc in next 3 sc, sc2tog) 5 times, sl st in first ch 1 to join—20 sts.

Rnd 14: Ch 1, (sc in next 2 sc, sc2tog) 5 times, sl st in first ch 1 to join—15 sts.

Rnd 15: Ch 1, (sc in next sc, sc2tog) 5times, sl st in first ch 1 to join—10 sts.

Rnd 16: Ch 1, (sc2tog) 5 times, sl st in first ch 1 to join—5 sts.

Rnd 17: Draw up a loop in each of 5 sc from prev rnd, yo and draw through all 5 loops together—1 st remains. Fasten off.

Chin Strap

Attach a doubled piece of gold metallic floss or yarn to the bottom of the hat. Make a crochet chain long enough to go under the chin of the doll. Fasten off and attach to the opposite side of the bottom of the hat.

FINISHING

Block lightly; weave in all ends. Stuff the hat with fiberfill (if desired) so that the hat maintains its shape.

Bonus Accessories to Crochet

Crochet Abbreviations

* . . . . .Repeat the instructions following the star the number of times indicated

() . . . . .Work the instructions within the parentheses the number of times indicated

[] . . . . .Work the instructions within the brackets the number of times indicated

beg. . . . . .beginning

ch. . . . . .chain stitch

dc . . . . .double crochet

hdc. . . . . .half double crochet

prev . . . . .previous

rem. . . . . .remaining

rep . . . . .repeat

rnd(s). . . . . .round(s)

RS . . . . .right side

sc. . . . . .single crochet

sc2tog . . . . .single crochet 2 stitches together

sk. . . . . .skip

sl st. . . . . .slip stitch

st(s). . . . . .stitch(es)

trc . . . . .triple crochet

WS . . . . .wrong side

yo . . . . .wrap the yarn around the hook